# Intr

Do you wonder if you hav
That you have been selected for something? A cause of a high
purpose?

Well you have been chosen and the why, when, where and how
is the subject of this book.

Your life isn't one of just survival through the daily grind of
life. The ups and downs of what you have been through are all for
a purpose. Every key experience you have had, every calamity that
befell you and each relationship that went south or well are part of
your overall story. Each major event in your life has been planned.

Have you felt this could be true? Was there even a hint of
recognition that certain events occurred for a purpose? And that
you were seemingly on a train headed for some unknown
destination and you couldn't get off?

This is because within your deepest thoughts, unconsciously,
you recognize that you are part of a greater plan. A plan that has
been drawn up with your improvement in mind.

There is an answer to your intuition and questions. The answer
is wonderful and your part in the drama you are leading is
fascinating. Once you realize the total environment in which you
reside in, you will recognize that your life is not dreary, but a heart
stopping adventure, a roller coaster ride that drives you forward
into an unimaginable future.

*Explore Your Destiny* is divided into four sections. Each
section supplies one more piece of the puzzle for you to place, so
you can look at your life's arc with new insights.

1.  Why – Why are we here and why must we live what we
    are living through right now? It's the age old
    expression, that we all say at one time or another, "Why
    me?" Well there is a reason and it will be explained to
    you.

2. When – In what period along your souls timeline is all of this happening? Yes, there is a greater context of your soul, which you may not be aware of. Knowing your relative position in the path to perfection will guide you to understanding your current life.

3. How – How does all of this occur? How does the entire process affect your destiny and actions? What are the rules of the game? Knowing the structure and comprehending the basic laws that direct your life provides you with a point of view that will put everything into perspective.

4. Where – Where is this world that plans our destiny? Are there good places to be and are there bad? Where does the earth fit into the logical structure? You will see where the regions that you are striving to attain are and where you may be living in your not-to-distant future.

I hope that after reading this book you will have a new view of your life. A view that allows you to look at your circumstances from afar and identify the turning points in your personal destiny. I want you to be in that high level observation tower where you can dispassionately evaluate your life and calmly proceed through the good and bad times. Always keeping your eye on the ball of what your true goal really is – Your triumph in the Spirit and Physical worlds.

Explore Your Destiny – Since Your Life's Path is (mostly) Predetermined

# Explore Your Destiny

Since Your Life's Path is (mostly) Predetermined

By

Brian Foster

http://www.nwspiritism.com/

1st Edition

# Table of Contents

# Section 1 – Why Do We Have a Fixed Set of Trials

How could there be a known future? A fixed event that shall transpire, even though a multitude of variables could sweep away any plan that a human could create. After all, how many of us have even the least desire followed. Our flimsiest constructs are regularly blown away like seeds in the wind. The answer must be because the future is immovable. Planned by higher powers than exist on the earth.

One could say, all of the prophecies that have been fulfilled are mere coincidences. That throughout history, we fool ourselves that something was foretold before the event occurred. But once we look into the detail, the area where people every day are experiencing some type of clairvoyance, it becomes harder to discard the idea, that somehow, someway, certain people are able to predict events which will occur in the future with great accuracy.

I was one of those who thought, that all fortune telling was mainly rewriting history after the fact, a refashioning of what was said to fit the facts that really transpired.

Until I was hit with indisputable proof that a prophecy could occur with uncanny accuracy. Then, I needed to find out how this could happen. Hence my journey into the realms of the spirit world began. At first I was going to write "my journey into the secrets of the spirit world", but that would be incorrect, for none of this has been deliberately hidden from us. It is all there out in the open. In books, in oral history, in traditions, still, at this moment, the message is being rained down upon us.

What has been hidden isn't because the spirit world has selected a few acolytes who would possess the knowledge and filter it out to us. No, the message has been shrouded because our culture represses any behavior or event that doesn't fit nicely with the narrative that no higher power can exists, except for our own scientifically proven theories. If we can't prove it today with our current set of instruments, then it doesn't exist and must be categorized as some sort of mental fantasy or failure.

A failure which could be easily explained if we could just spend more time investigating it, or that everyone should ignore it. It must be one of the two, never that there is indeed a universe surrounding ours, that interacts and guides us. That would be too fantastic to contemplate. Even if that phenomenon could provide the explanation for why we are where we are and what will be coming next, for all of us.

Finding the sources that lay open to anyone who scratches the surface, also led me to what is being told to thousands upon thousands of people all over the world today. Hourly, people in multiple countries and cultures are experiencing NDEs (Near Death Experiences) and reporting common themes.

As I investigated NDEs (Near Death Experiences), I found that many people received foreknowledge of events. Plus, they, with regularity, felt a common awareness of the love and complexity of the world beyond ours. A world which was vastly superior. A world which was interested in our development.

Repeatedly, reports would surface of a conversation about whether the subject of a NDE had learned enough to leave their physical body and return to the spirit world or should they return to absorb more of the lessons they were assigned. Or would their absence derail the trajectory of other lives.

Hence, this is why the word "pre-determined" is not quite adequate, it's more quasi-pre-determined, which isn't a word, at least the way I spell it, but which better conveys how our life actually works.

We have a road in which we should travel. There are guardrails and curbs to keep us on the path. Some drive slowly, never touching the sides; others barrel down at full speed. Scratching some paint along the way, but nevertheless maintaining their forward progress. But there are always some who career off the path, plow through whatever obstacles that may be placed in their way and rip to shreds their carefully laid out plans. Which, not only changes their life, but modifies the trajectories of others.

Therefore, Section 1 takes you through how and why I commenced my journey. What I now I believe and why others believe in a higher plane, a Supreme Intelligence, also commonly called God.

I review the common themes of NDEs and show how this intersects with Spiritism. I attempt to convey what is being communicated to us and how we are driven on by forces unseen, but felt in our daily lives. I expose why most people who experience NDEs have a vague recall of what they were told. Some can remember a few facts, but not others and why this is so.

Lastly, I delve into what is "Fate" and what power do we have to buck it or go with the flow. Plus, what are the important lessons and which may just be the time in between our assigned classes.

# Chapter 1 - How My Wife's NDE Made Me a Spiritist

I was not a spiritual person. I had a vague notion of a higher power, but one that really didn't care about us individually. After all, how could any power keep track of each and every one of us and determine what we had done in our lives. I had hopes of a life after death in heaven, but in reality, I expected that when we die, that is it. To me, the Bible was rather boring and ill written. I read and emulated the ancient Greeks and Romans more than our Western Civilization Christian traditions. From reading Plato, Livy, Cicero, and other ancient philosophers and writers, I believed that one should be honorable and truthful, even though I frequently failed at being so.

## My Wife's NDE

When my wife was seventeen years old, she had a bad accident, which caused her to lose a great deal of blood. She was taken to a hospital in Rio de Janeiro. She was delivered straight to the Emergency room, the doctor saw her and said, "Quickly we have to operate."

The nurse said, "But doctor, we don't have any anesthesia today."

The doctor replied, "Then we have to do without."

Ana said to herself, "God, I am ready to be taken."

Next, Ana noticed a lady, maybe a nurse, she was all in white, but the white seemed to radiate, who held her hand and told her that everything would be alright.

Ana's recollection was that surgery took just a moment, she heard the doctor say she would be discharged the next day. Ana did not feel any pain. She didn't see the lady who held her hand. The next day, her sisters told her the doctor thought she was on drugs, he was amazed she didn't cry out in pain.

When Ana arrived in her room, she saw another lady sitting down in the corner of the room, watching her, then the hospital room wall became transparent and she saw her life going by, like a movie. Ana didn't know at this time she had fallen into a coma.

As the movie played on, the lady in the corner communicated with her by speaking directly to Ana's mind. Eventually, Ana figured out that the movie was a movie of her life. Not only from the past, but it extended to her entire future, until her death. She saw her future marriage, building her house, scenes from a different hospital room in the future, the success of her children, everything. At the end the lady told her, "Bye, I am going back to my home." Ana asked, "Can't I go with you?" She replied, "Not now."

Overtime, the full memories of her trauma receded, but certain events would trigger flashbacks and bring to life particular scenes from her life's movie.

## My Spiritual Upbringing

Let me be clear upfront, my mother tried her best. My mother took me, my sister, and my father to church every Sunday. Of course, my sister seemed to like to dress up and wear her white gloves to church. My father went, mainly because he liked playing on the Church's baseball team. Although, he would complain that our Reverend didn't have the commitment to win, since he always tried to find playing time for everyone, not just the best, one of whom was my dad.

After the service, the young ones were taken to a Bible nursery school. I remember a group of us, this is when I was around five or six years old, we sat in a semi-circle, with the teacher and several of the mothers in front. Mine included. We read from a book, which had pictures of animals and a transparent picture of Jesus transposed over the illustrated bodies. The point of each page was to reinforce the idea that Jesus was inside all of us. At the end of each page, we would all say, "This is Jesus inside of the animal". Which was quite simple for me to do, since they had a picture of Jesus right over and partially inside each animal. Then, we got to the last page, on the page was one of those cheap mirrors that badly reflected our image. As I was the last person in the semi-circle, I had plenty of time to figure this one out.

Suddenly, the first child yelled out, "This is Jesus inside of me!" All of the mothers looked pleased at the successful teaching of this principle. One after another, the children would say the same thing, each time re-enforcing the correctness of thought and the spirituality that existed in each of the little darlings. By this time, I was thoroughly confused. What the heck were they seeing? Evidently, my book was special. The mirror did not lie.

When it came my turn, I yelled out, "It's me!" Was this the mark of a special destiny for me? That when others saw Jesus, I saw myself. I looked up and saw my mother put her hands on her face and bow her head down in shame, while the other mothers looked on with pity. My euphoria evaporated when I saw that all of the other books also had a mirror. My next thought was how could they have all been so wrong?

As I got older, my performance at church did not improve. I was a typical (well maybe atypical) active boy and if I got bored during the sermons, I would crawl under the pews. For some reason this did not go down well. But, the good news is that I really liked our Reverend. He was the nicest man in the world. Our two families would go to vacations at the beach together. Everyone at the church knew our families were friends.

When I was about ten or eleven, I was sitting in the pew with my mother waiting for our Reverend to walk down the aisle to start the service, I told my mom, "Look mom, God is coming!" Everyone laughed. I didn't know why, after all, he was a great guy and a wonderful person, wasn't he God? For reasons I have still not figured out, my mother gave up and let me stay home, with my dad, on Sundays. I will always cherish those wonderful Sundays, playing for hours with my army men.

As one can detect, my spiritual IQ was low to non-existent. I believed in facts and in what I could see. As I progressed in life, I did not change my outlook. I considered people who believed in spirits and ghosts to be mistaken and those who were very religious, to be people who needed a crutch to survive daily life.

## My Wife's Earlier Experience

Before my wife had her Near Death Experience, she had had a different type of revelation. When she was a young girl of 14, she went to her godmother's house to bring her some food, as she did on many occasions. This day was different, she told Ana to come close to her. Ana's godmother held her hands and began to tell of certain events that will happen in the future. She told her that she would marry a foreigner, meaning in this case a man who was not a Brazilian. After hearing about so many wondrous things that would happen to her, my future wife was very excited. After all, to a 14-year-old girl everything must happen rather quickly.

All through her twenties my wife waited for these foretold events to occur. She had worked for other people, even while she finished high school. She led a modest life in her small apartment. Gradually, the rhythm of daily life and the numerous encounters that gave rise to great hopes, which always led to failed expectations, allowed her to forget, or at least to suppress her memories of her godmother's talk and her time in a coma.

I met Ana in Rio de Janeiro, Brazil, when she was thirty-one. I had already been married once and had no wish to marry again. Little did I know that I was not in control of events, somehow, after meeting, we were married within eight months.

## Remembrances of the Future Foretold

When we got married, Ana spoke to me about her past experiences with her godmother and in the hospital. When I heard that Ana was told that she was destined to marry a foreigner, I just smiled and said to myself, "yes, right." I was condescending, I didn't believe a word, thinking these were just the product of superstition and wishful thinking.

But then, little hints would occur that there was more to this than pure fantasy. We went looking for a house, trudging through home after home as if trying to walk in a swamp. I was getting very bored with all of this, when we came to one house.

My wife said, "This is it!" I answered, "This is what?"

She told me this is the house where we were going to live. We called the real estate agent and made an offer, we were told that there were two offers on the table. I explained to my wife that we had a small to zero chance of getting that house.

"But", she said, "That house had three trees in the front! Just like my godmother told me."

"Ah", I replied very smugly, "The house actually has four trees in front."

"Nevertheless, we are going to buy that house." She retorted, with an air of superiority.

Somehow, the other two offers fell through and we purchased the house. As we moved in, I again pointed out the four trees in front. She merely looked at me, with that loving but slightly exasperated expression.

A month later, a wind storm blew through and knocked over one of the trees. I thought about it for a minute, but put it down to coincidence.

Other events would occur and afterward she would say, "Now I remember, my godmother told me that would happen." Again, I would always smile and say, "Of course, dear."

## The Improbable

Years past, and life went on. I was working for a bank, when the great recession started to form in 2006. The stock price of the bank started to drop. But I knew, the bank was financially healthy, after all, the entire senior management told us so. I had a conversation with Ana about the sub-prime business and how if many people couldn't pay their mortgages, other banks could be in trouble, but that we would be ok.

15

"Oh, now I remember," she said, "my godmother said you were going to work for a bank that would go bankrupt, but don't worry because you will still work for that bank, it will just change names."

What the heck was that! Impossible I said to myself. I dismissed what she said completely.

A month later, a well-connected firm took a part ownership in our financial institution. I thought that if they invested in us, with their association with the power brokers in DC and in Wall Street, we must be in a good position. I was so smart, I invested in more stock, hoping to make a large profit when we pulled through these troubles.

Four months later, the FDIC closed us, and I had lost everything. Or so I thought.

I came home and explained to my wife what happened. She said, "Don't worry, they will hire you back."

But, they didn't. I was given some months extra work to help transfer knowledge. At the end of that period I would be looking for a job in the worst financial crisis to hit the United States since the Great Depression.

At the end of my extension, I stated to look for a job. Again, my wife said, "Don't waste time looking for other jobs, they will hire you back."

What did she know? She didn't realize the extent of the catastrophe, I and millions others were all looking for those few positions.

I feverishly sought out work, after numerous fruitless interviews, in the end, after only being out of work for four months, I was hired back by the same bank, but with a different name.

# Quest for an Answer

I, who had always believed in free will, that I was a person who made my own destiny via my hard work, good choices and bad choices. For whatever happened to me, was caused by my actions or coincidence. Coincidence being the random events that may affect your life, while your life intersects with other people's lives. Plus, the randomness of natural occurrences, which may shape your life at times.

The improbably of an old women, who lived in practically a hut, with a thatched roof and earthen floors with chicks running around the floor inside the house (for I visited her once, when I first married Ana), could tell my wife thirty years ago, that the bank I worked for would go broke, change its' name and rehire me, was for all accounts an impossibility.

All I was left with, was the facts. If someone could perfectly forecast the future, then the future must be known by some power. My well-packaged belief system had been utterly destroyed. Stepped on by events.

I searched "destiny", "pre-destination", "fate", and everything related on the internet. I read many theories. One, which was interesting, is that all events our foretold, the Universe is like a grand DVD, in that you are able to select any moment and replay the scenes. This may be true, but the theory couldn't explain why or who caused this. From there, I researched the idea of the Universe being a giant hologram. Again, yes, it could be true, but why?

Then one day, I was watching the Brazilian channel Globo on cable TV, there was a program called "Fantastico", similar to our "60 Minutes". It was about Chico Xavier and his aptitude to communicate with spirits. His ability to write down what the spirits told him, the smallest details of deceased people's lives, all for the benefit of surviving family members. The facts he wrote down were investigated and found to be completely accurate. This was startling. I decided to read about him.

At an early age he communicated with his departed mother. In later life, a spirit, Emmanuel, told him that he would be used by the Spirit world to communicate with humanity. Chico was told to use the doctrine of Allan Kardec as his guide, and never stray off that path. Many people had tried to expose Chico as a fraud, but he said, "I will never fall down, because I never stood up.", meaning that of all the people he helped, plus the over 400 books he psychographed (written with his hand, but the spirits dictating), he gave all to charity, and he lived a very simple life.[1]

I decided to read about Spiritism and Allan Kardec. I found out that Spiritism was presented to us by the Spirit world so we here on earth may perfect ourselves and prepare the earth to reach a higher plane of existence. Utilizing Spiritism, we are expected to improve our collective behavior. Spiritism was brought to us via the work of Allan Kardec.

In 1857, in response to the growing interest in spirits and mediums, Allan Kardec (pen name of the French teacher and educator Hippolyte Léon Denizard Rivail) organized a series of questions designed to discern the exact nature and wishes of the spirits. He did not accept information from just one medium, but verified the response to a question from multiple mediums throughout Europe.[2] Allan Kardec wrote a total of five books documenting the answers to his questions. The basic tenets of Spiritism are:

1. Love God.

2. Do unto others as you would have others do unto you.

3. Practice justice.

4. Forgive all who offend you.

5. Make amends for our own wrong doing.

The spirits revealed to us the basic facts of our existence:

1. Your soul is immortal.

2. You travel through multiple lives as a process to learn to love, be fraternal, and be selfless.

3. The goal of God is for every spirit to one day be pure.

4. There is no eternal hell, it is a station for souls who are materialistic and have an excessive love of self. Eventually, each spirit will learn selflessness and ascend.

5. There are many levels of heaven. Heaven is not a place where we have eternal leisure, but one of on-going work to help others.

6. Life on earth is like a school. You are assigned events in your life and how you react and behave will determine your spiritual progress.

The last point struck me like a lightning bolt. The series of trials in our lives are proscribed, we must march on through our assigned tribulations. In that our life is pre-destined, but we do have free will in the choices and our attitudes during those trials. Oh, I wish I had learned these truths earlier, I wouldn't have been so full of self-pity. I wished I could have met my adversities like a true gentleman, but of course I failed.

While many other precepts of Spiritism coincide with other religions, the principle of karma and multiple lives, but nothing else explained the entire process of the injustice and seemingly incomprehensible tragedies that befall innocent people. The maimed, those born with disabilities, gentle and wonderful lives cut short, all apparently without true cause. But, there is a true cause, and in many cases the people so afflicted asked for their right to pay their redemption, seeking a path to learn to be better spirits.

## My Life as a Spiritist

I am reading and re-reading Allan Kardec's books and I am slowly absorbing the books that have been translated into English,

19

which were psychographed by Chico Xavier. The novels dictated to Chico by the Spirit Emmanuel are full of fresh insights into our behavior and the subtle manipulations on our lives by the Spirit world. While the books inspired by Andre Luiz directly open a portal into the process and the amount of assistance given to us by the Spirit world.

I wish I could say my life now is one full of bliss and understanding. It is not, but I am learning, slowly to control my temper and my baser instincts. I am still trying to not judge people at a glance, not to dismiss those I deem unimportant. I desire to see all of humanity as my fraternity, I am trying, and alas the old habits are hard to break. I shall not give up. I shall continue to pray for guidance and the power to correct myself.

Lastly, I have embarked on distilling the essence of what I have discovered to enable others to learn about their life at a much earlier time then I had the privilege to. With my books and my blog, I wish to create a comfortable portal through which one can serenely evaluate their life and feel the sense of peace and love that come with knowing that you are part of a grand design.

# Chapter 2 - The Intersection of NDE (Near Death Experience) and Spiritism

Along with my personal discovery of Spiritism, I researched the phenomena of people's near death experiences. The stories that were told fitted the incident of my wife in her episode. This was another revelation for me; the fact that countless others had similar visits from a world beyond must signal a greater meaning.

There has been numerous stories about NDE's (Near Death Experiences) since mankind have been on earth, but with the advent of the internet, the gathering and discussion of people's experiences has reached a new level. To the people visiting the other world and writing about NDE's, their conception of the order of the Universe and their place within it have undergone a transformation. The knowledge that they really have a soul and it lives beyond their physical body brings a whole new set of questions. These questions are answered by Spiritism.

In fact, the explosion of interest in the entire NDE phenomenon could act as a catalyst for all us to reconnect with our spiritual side. A chance to rebalance our materialistic side with our spiritual needs.

Some of the recent NDE stories published on the nderf.org (Near Death Experience Research Foundation) site, underline the sense of otherworldliness and provides motivation to explore the state of the universe in which our spirit lives.

"While I was on the stretcher I observed a very white light at a distance, which I was approaching, I was like floating in the air." – Victorio from Argentina, published in March, 2014[3]

"This unfolding of pictures and gaps developed and progressed continuously, presenting a constant delicate consequential line in perfect order, a chain of events, yet somehow they were all happening at once. The past the present and the future were all happening at once. It was inspiring to witness the order and sense that all these little pictures seemed to have in "the big picture". I felt a lot of compassion. I was all forgiven. In fact there was nothing to forgive. I could see that my life had "perfect order" to it. In some way it was like watching a mathematical equation or sum that makes perfect sense- such event and such event create this kind of result. It was a simple portrayal of natural cause and effect with a gentle understanding." – Romy from Australia, published in March, 2014[4]

People experiencing NDEs write about meeting spirits and communicating with deceased family members, as Fabio, from Italy, "I 'feel' a presence, something, someone, I can't explain it. I saw nothing and heard no word, nevertheless, I suddenly realize that the 'speaker' had always been there, and had followed me while I was in the tunnel, and somehow he had perhaps helped me to turn back. We began a silent dialogue. An immense and unconditional love. A flow of love."[5]

Who are these other beings and how can we talk with family members long gone from the earth? Does our spirit only live once in a physical body or do we truly travel through multiple lives? Many religions and individuals believe in the concept of reincarnation. Reincarnation provides a framework for the existence of an immortal soul and a reason why we are truly reborn. People, who had no religious beliefs before, upon reviving from NDE's have returned accepting their soul to be immortal and that reincarnation is a necessary process for our quest to become a better and more loving individual.

Kevin Williams, who works on the www.near-death.com website, has complied and quoted parts of a research paper by Amber Wells, in her article she highlights the following:

"The majority of experiencers mentioned learning or enlightenment as the main purpose underlying reincarnation. Here are some comments by experiencers:

"The spirit needs to embody itself in matter to experience it and learn. There are karmic patterns to learn lessons and to work spirit in matter."

"Life itself is a series of learnings. The lessons are universal, the two most important being truth and forgiveness."

"We progress at our own rate to reach the light. If you do things that take you away from the light, then you are perpetuating your time here."

"The inner quality is there, the inner self remains, but the external aspect that may have seemed very strong is dissolved. Individuality wasn't the same there. It was the same as everybody and everybody was me. Your spirit is always you. You are not the personality that you are on Earth. In the other realm you are everything, light is everything."[6]

The findings and comments above have all been explained by the doctrines of Spiritism. The people who have traveled through a NDE knew what they experienced, but now they have a name for the entire construct of the universe in which they entered for that brief period of time.

As one can see, the statements presented in Amber Well's paper, such as, "Life itself is a series of learnings. The lessons are universal, the two most important being truth and forgiveness", have also been delivered to us via an alternative channel. That of the Spirit world communicating directly to mediums to alert us of a life beyond our single human existence.

# The View from the Other Side

The view of our experiences from the Spirit world can be discovered in the books by Allan Kardec and Chico Xavier. Allan Kardec, in his book *The Spirits Book*, documents, by a series of questions and answers, what happens during the separation of the body and the soul:

*154. Is the separation of the soul from the body a painful process?*

"No; the body often suffers more during life that at the moment of death, when the soul is usually unconscious of what is occurring to the body. The sensations experienced at the moment of death are often a source of enjoyment for the spirit, who recognizes them as putting an end to the term of his exile."

*155. How is the separation of soul and body effected?*

"The bonds which retained the soul being broken, it disengages itself from the body."

*Is this separation effected instantaneously, and by means of an abrupt transition? Is there any distinctly marked line of demarcation between life and death?*

"No; the soul disengages itself gradually. It does not escape at once from the body, like a bird whose cage is suddenly opened. The two states touch and run into each other; and the spirit extricates himself, little by little, from his fleshly bonds, which are loosed, but not broken." [7]

These statements were written in the 1850's, well before the formal documentation of NDE's arrived. Doesn't the above fit perfectly with the sensation of the spirit somewhat free of the body, communicating with and seeing other spirits, but still connected? All who have had a NDE still had a bond with their body, otherwise they would not have been able to return to their physical form. Death is only the destruction of our body, our soul is immortal.

In Allan Kardec's book, Heaven and Hell, an evocation is being held at a Mortuary chamber on April 23, 1862. The participants are communicating with Mr. Sanson, who was a member of the Parisian Spiritist Society, he died on April 21, 1862. He had spent a year in suffering before his death and he expressed the wish to be communicated with after his death. Here are some of the excerpts:

*7. Did you retain your awareness up to the last instant?*

"Yes, my spirit retained its faculties. I no longer saw; I foresaw. My entire life unfolded within my memory and my last remembrance, my dying request, was to be able to communicate with you as I am doing right now. I next asked God to watch over you so that the dream of my life could be fulfilled."

*8. Were you conscious at the moment in which your body breathed its last? What happened to you at that time? What sensations did you feel?*

"Life expires and sight, or rather, the spirit's sight darkens. You find yourself in the void, the unknown, and then as if carried by an unknown power, you find yourself in a world where all is joy and wonder. I no longer felt anything, nor was I sure about what was occurring: nevertheless, an ineffable happiness surrounded me and I no longer felt the grip of pain."[8]

Again, the same sensations, the same feelings of love and joy. There is a book, *Workers of the Life Eternal*, which was dictated to Chico Xavier in 1946, by the spirit Andre Luiz, which describes a death experience from the point of view of one of the spirit helpers in facilitating a person's passing over to the Spirit world. Andre was assigned to a team of spirits who are to assist a man named Dimas to complete his life. Dimas' mother, is also there in spirit to help her son in his first moments back in the Spirit world. The chapter on Dimas tells of the Spirit helpers preparing him for the final transition:

"Dimas-discarnate was now hovering a few inches above Dimas-corpse, attached to his body only by a thin, silvery cord similar to a delicate elastic thread between the abandoned brain of dense matter and the brain of rarefied matter of the liberated organism.

Dimas' mother quickly left the material body and gathered up the new form, wrapping it in a pure white tunic that she had brought with her.

To our incarnate friends, Dimas was completely dead. To us, though, the operation was not yet complete. The Assistant determined that the fluidic cord should remain intact until the following day, taking into account the needs of the "dead man", who was not yet fully prepared for a quicker disengagement.

And while the doctor was providing technical explanations to the sobbing relatives, Jeronimo invited us to leave, while entrusting the newly discarnate soul to the care of the woman who had been his devoted mother in the physical world."[9]

The act of dying is not a solitary experience, but one in which the Spirit world actively assist us. The writings of the Spirit world reinforces and provides an independent validation of the findings of the research into NDE experiences. In fact, Spiritism provides the context, the reason, and the motivation for our life here on earth.

Within this book, I shall present more NDE stories and interpret them according to the Spiritist Doctrine so you may determine for yourself how the collective experiences of thousands of people who have lived through a NDE may be part of a spiritual awakening.

# Chapter 3 - Why Our Memoires of NDE's are Imprecise

When people experience NDE's, many have the future revealed to them. For some, they speak about the future while delirious, others see the future while in a NDE state, then forget most of what they saw. Why do many of the memories of NDEs disappear or fade away so quickly. There is a reason why we must forget and it is fully explained by Spiritism.

In the book, *Between Heaven and Earth*, dictated to Francisco C. Xavier, by the spirit Andre Luiz, a woman, named Antonina, is given a chance to meet her deceased child (Marcos) in the spirit world. She finds the child is happy with his life in heaven. She feels wonderful about the experience. When her spirit is put back into her body, the team leader (Clarencio), with whom Andre and Hilario are assisting, says:

"Our friend cannot hold on to the memory of what occurred," stated Clarencio.

"Why not?" asked Hilario.

"Very few spirits are capable of living on earth with the visions of life eternal. They need the environment of inner twilight. A full memory of what occurred would result in a fatal longing."

But the Minister patiently explained: "Each stage in life is characterized by special purposes. Honey may be tasty nectar for the child, but it mustn't be given indiscriminately - too much and it becomes a laxative. While we are in the earthly envelope, we cannot stay in contact with the spirit realm too long or our soul will lose interest in struggling worthily till the end of the body. Antonina will recall our trip but only vaguely, like someone who brings a beautiful but blurry picture to the living arena of her soul. But she will remember her son more vividly, enough for her to feel reassured and convinced that Marcos is waiting for her in the Greater Life. Such certainty will be sweet nourishment for her heart."[10]

The message we are hearing is that contact with the spirit realm is too enjoyable, a feeling of peacefulness and love that we would constantly long for, if we remembered its existence. One of the recurring themes of NDEs is the person who is in contact with the spirits, tells them that they wish to stay and not return to their life on earth, but are in the end told, "You must go back. It is not your time yet." Hannah F. who wrote about her NDE in April, 2014, supplies a perfect example. She describes the wonderment, the beauty, and the vague memories of a conversation:

"There was a waterfall in front of us and beautiful scenery. I would probably call it a beautiful garden however everything was natural. I remember a feeling of love and reassurance. I don't remember what the man was telling me about but he was speaking for a long time. It felt like hours. I remember being shocked at a few things he said.

Now, in my experience I was ME but i wasn't "HANNAH". I knew myself but not as Hannah. I don't remember what was spoken but I remember the feelings I felt. All I remember him saying was, "it's time to go back now." I looked at him puzzled (Not remembering earth) and then felt a pain on my shoulder. When I felt the pain I began to travel through a tunnel. As I went down the tunnel I could see images of my life and my life on earth came back to me."[11]

Notice the fuzzy knowledge of the exact events, a feeling of an interesting conversation, a good time, but a recollection as if you drank just a little too much and couldn't remember the great bar conversation you had last night. The one certainty, was that a better place was visited. Therefore, if we actually are a spirit, why aren't we allowed memories of our past lives, on earth and in the spirit world?

### Forgetfulness of the Past - Why?

When we reincarnate, we are not allowed to remember our past lives or our time as a spirit on earth. To determine why this is so,

28

let's examine a case of a spirit who was reincarnated with the ability to remember past lives. In the book, *The Messengers*, psychographed by Francisco C. Xavier, dictated to him by the spirit Andre Luiz, Andre encounters a person who completely failed in their mission on earth. Joel, the spirit who laments his failure, tells Andre:

"My failure was not because of too much sensitivity, but because of how I used it. As I understand now, God allows some individuals to have superior sensitivity so they can use it as a tool, a kind of powerful magnifying lens that helps them see the right course of life for themselves and others they are supposed to help. This extra sensitivity can help to perceive life's path, identify dangers and shortcuts, and clearly see obstacles. Instead of using the gift in that way, all I did was use it to satisfy my warped curiosity about myself."

"To fulfill my role of helping others, my expanded perception included the ability to remember my past lives. Most people can't recall their own past, and for good reason. In my case, I was supposed to use that knowledge in my service to help others, not to obsess about it, and that's where I failed."

"I began to obsess about a previous existence in which I has been Monsignor Alejandre Pizarro who participated in the last years of the cruel Spanish Inquisition. That's when I started misusing the spiritual magnifying lens I told you about. The excitement of the sensations was inebriating – it was as if I was addicted to drugs or alcohol – and I neglected all of my previously accepted responsibilities."

"I started spending all of my time trying to locate the people who had been my companions during my time centuries before as a religious man. I forced myself to find each and every one of them in space and time, reconstituting their biographical sketches, completely ignoring the work I was supposed to do."[12]

"So I spent my life in this fashion – going from revelation to revelation, sensation to sensation. I, who had reincarnated with the unusual ability to remember in order to be useful transformed my gift into a tool of addiction. I'd thrown away an opportunity to redeem myself, and I lived tortured by intermittent bouts of hallucination. The misuse of my sensitivity generated an imbalance in my mind so that I became painfully unstable."[13]

A perfect example of what could happen when we know too much and are unable to focus on what we need to learn. Imagine sitting in a classroom, with the TV blaring, showing you scenes from your previous existence while at the same time attempting to comprehend the basic facts of Algebra. One could not possess the mental force to concentrate on that valuable lesson, especially if you had had some type of mathematics background before and tried to merge it with what you are learning at the present time. Not only would you reject parts of what were offered to you, but you would be exasperated with having to sit through this lecture again, even though spaced out by hundreds of years.

There are other reasons as well, in *The Gospel According to Spiritism*, it says, "A spirit is frequently reborn into the same environment in which it has already lived, and finds itself in relationships with the same individuals in order to repair the evil it did to them. If it were to recognize in them those whom it used to hate, perhaps its hatred would reawaken. In any case, it would feel humiliated in the presence of those it offended."[14] Therefore, the need to forget the past, not only in our present life, but from other lives is a necessity to be able to learn and to forgive others and to grow spiritually.

But, are we a completely blank slate, always starting over? No, for again in *The Gospel According to Spiritism*, we are told, "God has given us for our advancement precisely what is necessary and what will be enough for us: the voice of conscience and our instinctive tendencies, taking from us what could harm us."[15] The underlines are mine. These are the two main levers of our behavior. If our conscience (or instinct) tells us something is wrong, I suggest it is doing so with the wisdom of hundreds, if not thousands, of years of experience behind it.

30

Hence, we do retain traces of our past lives, which are very important parts of our daily life. We take our instincts and our conscience for granted, not realizing that we have been developing these tools for numerous lives. Ponder your thoughts as you determine the best course of action and feel what is the right thing to do, as opposed to the action that may bring you immediate gratification, understand that your action will have consequences far in the future. Do you really want that extra cash now, but pay for a severe trial in the future, so you will learn, down to the foundation of your heart, that you should always do the right thing? Because, according to Spiritism, you will be sent on trials, programmed to improve your deficiencies, until you fully absorb the intended lesson. And you thought childhood was tough!

# Chapter 4 - Fate, Destiny, Determinism – None of That – You are Just Going to the School of Earth

Now that we know that we are immortal spirits who reincarnate on earth, while our memories of past lives are hidden from us, what is the plan for us? Why have we been be sent back to earth? Is there a set course we must follow? Attempting to determine what is fate and what is freewill is difficult when exploring Spiritism. This chapter explains the areas of your life that must occur and the areas where you have a choice.

Discovering Spiritism leads one to the feeling that you are on a roller coaster and are unable to get off. The more you read, the more questions you have, then you try and find where they could be answered, but at the end you have a larger set of questions than when you started. The numerous questions could be separated into major categories. One of the most significant set of inquiries concerns the matter of your personal destiny. The discussion of the plan for your life on earth is scattered throughout Kardec's books and in psychographed books by mediums, such as Francisco C. Xavier. This chapter pulls together different sources to present to you an introduction of the basic principles and concepts that have dictated your life's plan.

In Allan Kardec's *The Gospel According to Spiritism*, the starting point for understanding your trials is in this paragraph, "Christ said, 'Blessed are the afflicted, for they shall be comforted'. But how can we bless suffering if we don't know why we suffer? Spiritism shows that the cause lies in previous existences and in the destiny of earth, where humans expiate their past. It shows them the purpose of their suffering as being salutary which lead to healing and which are the purification that ensures happiness in future existences. Humans understand that they deserve to suffer and they find suffering to be just. They know that this suffering aids their progress and they accept it without complaining, just as workers accept the work that will ensure their wages."[16]

Why is it important to understand our place in our destiny? According to the quote above, we should gladly accept whatever is thrown at us with a smile and work our butts off to get through it. Well, except for the few of us that possess that perfect attitude of accepting all of life's vicissitudes, we need to first comprehend what is occurring so we can meditate on it and try to mold our attitude so we may survive the ordeal the best that we can.

First the good news. We do have freewill. Although, I believe it is less than what is advertised. Why, because the spirit world wants all of us charging ahead in life as well as we are able. And after all, you want to keep the troops motivated, don't you? The bad news is that you will be paying for your transgressions in past lives; there is no escaping that fact. So here is the hard part, how do you combine the expiation of your sins with making free-will choices and doing what you desire in your life?

In the book, *Missionaries of Light*, psychographed by Francisco C. Xavier, where Andre Luiz (the spirit author of the book) is discussing the imminent birth of a spirit (Segismundo), who will undergo trials for his past sins. Andre asks about the plan for the spirit's life. Alexandre, Andre's teacher at the moment, replies, "Notice that I said benefit and not destiny. Many people confuse a constructive plan with fatalism. Both Segismundo and our brother Herculano have the information we are talking about, because nobody enters a school for a more or less long period without a specific purpose and without knowing the rules that he or she should obey".[17]

We are all assigned a curriculum, a course of study in the college campus that suits our needs for our present life. A learning institution that is intended to move us to a higher level. A higher level only if we are able to accumulate enough credits, or we may be required to repeat.

Andre probes deeper into the contours of the plan for Segismundo. Andre wishes to know how the trials are matched up with the past sins in Segismundo's future life and receives further information from Alexandre, "For that reason the diagram of useful trials is drawn up beforehand, much like a student's work book at a regular school. In view of this, the diagram corresponding to Segismundo has been duly drawn up, taking in consideration the physiological cooperation of his parents, the domestic backdrop and the fraternal assistance that will be given to him by countless friends from this side. So, imagine our friend returning to a school – earth – and in doing so fulfilling a purpose; to acquire new qualities. In order to do this, he will have to submit to the rules of the school, renouncing up to a point the great freedom he used to enjoy in our environment."[18]

Hearing this, Andre is confused, he believes Alexandre's description implies a fixed destiny, since a detailed plan is formulated and all external events seemingly factored into the plan. Alexandre corrects him:

"Don't fall into the error assumed by many people. That would imply an obligatory form of spiritual conduct. Of course, individuals are reborn with a relative independence and are sometimes subjected to certain harsher conditions for educational purposes, but such imperative never suppresses the free impulse of the soul in its aim toward advancement, stagnation or fall into lower conditions. There is a plan of spiritually edifying tasks to be fulfilled by spirits who reincarnate, where their guides set the approximate quota of eternal qualities that they are prone to acquire during their transitory existence. The spirit who is returning to the physical realm can either improve this quota and surpass its superior's predictions by means of its own intensive efforts or it can fall short and go further into debt to its neighbor, scorning the holy opportunities that had been granted it."[19]

Therefore, we should think of our life like we are at school, a school we can't possibly escape until we graduate. Graduation is death, but don't think about that right now! In that school, we have classes we like and others that we either detest or find extremely boring. In most cases we sit and dread the possibility of being called to answer. Like all things, the bell eventually rings and we move on to the next class. We don't have the freedom to leave the school or the classroom for the time allocated to the subject. But we do have the freedom to either raise our hand and answer correctly, with enthusiasm or slink in the back and mutter incomprehensively, hoping to escape that moment of terror. Guess which one gets you the better grade?

## What Can You Do About It?

How should you handle difficult times? Periods of life where nothing seemingly works and there are no ladders to escape? Again, Alexandre gives the answer, "Every plan that is drawn up in the higher spheres has the good and ascension as its basic objectives, and every soul that reincarnates, even one that finds itself in apparent desperate conditions, has resources to continue to improve."[20] Therefore, first feel certain that you do have the means to successively climb out of whatever problem you are in.

There are two important actions you can accomplish, in any situation, one is to remember the golden rule, the basis of Spiritism, "Do unto others and you would have them do unto you"; in fact go further and actively help others if at all possible. The second is to maintain a positive attitude. In the book, *Action and Reaction*, again inspired by the spirit Andre Luiz, psychographed by Francisco C. Xavier, Andre wishes to know how an utterly bad spirit has any chance to improve themselves while they are in a difficult trial on earth. He receives this answer:

> "Let's imagine a monstrous criminal who has been segregated in a prison. Accused of many crimes, he has been deprived of any of the freedom he would experience in an ordinary cell. Even in this condition, if he were to use his time in prison to willingly work for the well-being of the authorities and his fellow inmates, accepting with humility and respect the decisions of the law that is used to correct him – such attitude being the result of his free will to help or harm himself – in a short time this prisoner would begin to attract the sympathy of those about him, thus advancing surely toward self-regeneration".[21]

What we are being told is that the constraints of our fate is of our own making. Certain events and trials we must live through, our only freedom is our attitude and love for others during these times. The less we have to pay for past sins, the more freedom we gain to make choices to improve our souls.

For those in the midst of painful trials, pray for help and forgiveness, but above all else maintain a positive outlook and love and care for others. By this you will have paid your debt and exceeded the expectations of those that created your plan.

### How to Prepare for Future Trials

How do you build up the required strength to survive future trials? As in school, where there are periods between classes, there are periods between trials. These are the times to learn about Spiritism, participate in charity work and ponder on why you have gone through the occurrences of your life so far. In the book, *Action and Reaction*, Andre learns about a man who at forty committed suicide. He learns that after years of suffering in the spirit world, the man is reincarnated. Andre is told that as part of the man's trials he will have an "overwhelming temptation to commit suicide again at the exact age in which he forsook his responsibilities the previous time".[22]

So, think carefully when you have great events in your life. Contemplate about how you must have made the wrong decision in a previous existence and what steps you can take to improve. Andre asks how can this unfortunate man resist the lure the second time? He learns that, "If this man has not saved up renewing and educational resources through learning and the practice of fraternity so as to overcome the inevitable crisis, it will be very hard for him to avoid committing suicide again because, despite being reinforced from the outside, temptations have their starting point within us and they feed on what is already there".[23]

This is not a new trial, but a chance for a retest. If you have studied hard and learned to live with others as you should, you will pass the test. After you live through it, rejoice in the knowledge that you won't have to live through this type of event ever again.

Our destiny, our course of study in our school on earth, is not supposed to be tranquil, if it was you wouldn't be able to advance. Take comfort that which you believe are tough lessons are nothing compared to what truly failed spirits must experience. Pray for those who are in the middle of justly difficult lessons and learn to travel through yours with a constructive viewpoint. Graduation from the school of life is indeed death, which if you fully passed all of your classes could mean you are finished with earthly universities, but at least the reward for good grades in most classes is an even more fascinating life the next time and an exciting and fulfilling job in the spirit world before its back to the campus.

# Chapter 5 - NDE – Near Death Experience – James

James had a full life review, with a council determining if he should stay or return. He also found out that indeed, he did have a life plan.

James had major surgery. During his operation his heart stopped and he was guided to the spirit world. There, he was brought in front of a tribunal, to determine if he should return or not to his physical life. You can read his whole story at the NHNE Near Death website. The direct link to James' story is http://nhneneardeath.ning.com/profiles/blogs/my-nde-2.

When James' heart stopped, a woman spirit approached him and led him out of our world to the spirit world. Where, as many others before him have noted, the flowers and trees shined as if lit from within. In the many books psychographed by Francisco C. Xavier, the spirits who communicate with us, also comment on the wondrous aspects of the light, how their senses are heighten and everything takes on a brilliant hue, with colors that we have never seen before.

James then describes where his life would be reviewed:

"I was led by the lady through the forest. I asked where we were, what had happened to me, where were we going. I was told everything was fine and my questions would be answered soon. I didn't feel concerned in fact I felt calm and Peaceful. I was led by the lady to a clearing in the forest in the middle of which was a large wooded oval table with 10 or 11 people seated around it and one chair empty which I was indicated to sit at. Then the lady left. The people at the table seemed very familiar, but in an 'other' worldly way and also had the same young but old looking qualities. I was warmly welcomed and told that I had left my physical body, and the purpose of the council was to decide if I should stay or return to it, and that a review would take place to determine this. The review consisted of a screen which appeared above the table in the center which began to play a 'film' of my life from the moment I was born. Members of the council paused the film at different parts and we looked at the circumstances surrounding specific events, sometimes from the different perspectives of the other people involved, but mostly they were interested in how the experiences had affected me, and my feelings about things." [24]

As on earth, in the spirit world we all have our group of friends. Friends who have been with us since we were in school and who have always been concerned with our welfare; constantly checking on our progress, with the noble aim of assisting us in our major life challenges. We have our friends in the spirit world, who are all the more special because sometimes they watch over us and other times they reincarnate to share our trials together.

Additionally, we all have mentors, older and wiser people who we look for advice and guidance. Again, the same concept applies to our spiritual mentors. The group that worked with James is most probably made up of friends and mentors, souls that he has intimately known before, but due to his recent separation from his body, his memory before the commencement of his current physical life is hazy. Hence, he seems to know them and feels comfortable in their presence.

Next, James' life is reviewed. And not just his actions, but the emotional affect he had upon others and the motivations that caused his actions are analyzed. This is one of the central tenets of Spiritism, our thoughts are actions, for with thoughts all begins and actions are merely the completion of a plan. It gets more complex, for our very thoughts influence events and others around us. We are all like radio towers, beaming our innermost musings and emotional highs and lows to all around us. The spirit world tells us we have a responsibility to control the waves emanating from our brains.

This all sounds extremely difficult to perform, but think about why this must be so for a moment. As we progress and become higher and pure spirits, the power of our minds also increase in force. Therefore, to ascend in the ranks of the spirits, we must learn to control that which shall, in the future, possess great power.

James then tells us about the analysis of his life to date:

"The experience was uncomfortable at times, I had to see myself warts and all, I saw the best and the worst in myself. But never at any time did I feel I was being judged by anyone present. We reached my present circumstances and I saw that my lung condition had been created by myself to give me an exit opportunity. We had a long debate after the film about my life blueprint and whether or not I had fulfilled my chosen experiences which were mostly linked to previous lifetimes and spiritual 'baggage' that needed to be cleared and healed. I felt that I needed more time on earth and this was agreed by the council, who also told me that I would need to go back more spiritually awake to accomplish this."[25]

James understands completely the reason for his life on earth when he writes the words, "life blueprint". First, this proves that James is an advanced spirit, for spirits that exist on the lower planes, who aren't interested in improving themselves, are arbitrarily assigned their station, appearance and trials in life. While those who are actively attempting to overcome the deficiencies they detected in their being, focus on repairing those holes in their next life and participate in laying out the plan for their time on earth in great detail.

There are many instances of this in Spiritist literature. One example is of a man who committed suicide in a previous life, abandoning his wife and children to destitution, and is planning his next life. In the book, *Memoirs of a Suicide*, he tells of his "blueprint":

"I won't be able to have children! By not looking after my family; by rejecting, half way through, the honorable responsibility of being head of the household in order to help me ascend in merit. I put myself in the wretched position of not being granted the chance of building a family and being a

40

father again in my next existence!"[26]

Hence, James is but one example of a person planning to overcome what they failed in their previous life. Therefore, the trials that we select, or to put it in a different manner, the classes in the school of earth that we register for, are all required prerequisites in our quest to become higher spirits. At some point in the future, we will attain that goal and no longer need to wear our earthly clothes.

Another fascinating comment made by James is his mentioning that his lung condition was pre-planned. How can that be? Well, again, this is not uncommon in the spiritual world. Not only do we determine the complete diagram of our bodies, but we also plan in advance afflictions that await us. In the book, *Missionaries of the Light*, by Francisco C. Xavier, inspired by the spirit Andre Luiz, Andre talks to a spirit who works in the Reincarnation Planning Center in the heavenly city Nosso Lar. He points out the extent of our future planning:

> "Here is the plan for the future reincarnation of a friend of mine. Do you see some dark spots from the descending colon to the sigmoid loop? This indicates that he will suffer from a large ulcer in this area as soon as he becomes an adult. Nevertheless, he has chosen it."[27]

The extent of the details that are invested in planning for our corporeal experiences is truly astonishing. Therefore, no one should take their life lightly, for countless hours of dedication were devoted to preparing our entry into our campus called Earth.

James recovered from his operation and returned to the land of the living. But he was a changed man. He trained as a Hypnotherapist and became a Past Life Therapist, focusing on the time spans between physical existences. As was determined by the council that judged him, he was given increased spiritual powers, which enabled him to begin assisting others in their own spiritual awakening.

James talks about his increased sensitivity:

"After my NDE, and once I was working with myself spiritually I started having out of body experiences. At first I would 'awake' from sleep to find myself watching myself sleep! then I began to leave my body and go to the spirit realms where I met my spirit guides and also people I have known who have passed from the earth; my grandparents, people who I had cared for in my work. My spirit guides began to 'educate' me about the different states of existence that a soul passes through in its great journey through creation, and also to show me things that would come to pass on the earth, how the earth would change and become less dense than it is now."[28]

All of James' NDE is explained and given context by the Doctrine of Spiritism. Spiritism reveals to us that we are all immortal spirits, striving to improve; that we must control our selfish and materialistic tendencies to be more loving, fraternal and spiritual. We are on earth to help others also ascend.

The spirit world is the real world, where our family resides. Families that have been reincarnated in different permutations through multiple generations. Always at our sides and constantly reaching out to be of assistance.

Spiritism is guiding the entire human race to a better place. As written in the books by Allan Kardec, the codifier of Spiritism; the earth will change. Currently, the earth is a planet of atonement, where immature spirits live to learn and to pay for their past mistakes. In the future, the earth will be a planet of regeneration, where there will live more good souls than bad and selfishness, jealousy, and wars are a thing of the past. Our bodies will become lighter, for as our spirits advance our ties to the physical world become less dense, hence our temporary human casings no longer need the brute force to survive in a savage world.

# Section 2 – When Will Our Trials Occur and When Will We be done

Now that we understand our life's path is constrained, we need to discover when is our fate determined. At what point before we are thrust into this world is the spirit world actively planning our campaign for betterment.

Since we face multiple reincarnations, we should be aware of our current stage of maturity. Spirits start out as primitive beings that require repeated lives to be able to exist in a semi-civilized society. Next we graduate to worlds of atonement, whereby whenever we commit wrongs, we must pay for these in our next life.

As we matriculate we begin to build a foundation of knowledge and attitudes that are meant for us to use in the next life. Constructing an ever greater sphere of love and wisdom is our constant goal. Hence, we must understand the process of reincarnation and how we play our part in the great purifying process of our soul.

This section is meant to be a quick primer on reincarnation and its ramifications. I have a book, *The Case for Reincarnation – Your Path to Perfection*, which covers in great detail all facets from planning your existence, selecting your body, the events that will shape your development, to the diseases that you chose to suffer through in later life.

What is necessary to convey in this section is the enormous sweep of your life. When you are a child you think what it would be like to be grown up, able to make your own decisions. Travel where you wish and be with who you desire.

For as a child or a teenager we are bound to the parameters given to us. Our circle is carefully drawn by those wiser entities, our parents. Our friends, attitudes and thoughts are analyzed for errors and plans are made for corrective actions.

We, who are here on earth at this moment, are in the same position. We are not allowed to wander according to our free-will. We are not permitted out of a carefully designed sphere. While the sphere is huge, according to our small point of view, the universe inhabited by the spirit world is beyond our imagination.

As we tell our children, don't chafe under our rules for soon enough you shall be an adult and can do what you want, we are in a similar situation. The difference is that we must understand what it means to be immortal. For it is different than the vision of entering adult life, it is the realization that we have to carefully form our capabilities and thoughts to ascend to the pantheon of pure spirits who direct our early lives.

We need to feel the love in which we are guided and to acknowledge the time and effort put into our pursuit of perfection. The amount of energy expended on our behalf should not be underestimated. Imagine the years of schooling to form a responsible immortal spirit, which wouldn't just be twelve years of school with four more years of college, but tens of thousands to possible hundreds of thousands of years of training. From being forged in the harshest conditions, such as drilling soldiers in live combat on mountain tops to the opposite of gaining the taste of living in luxury, lording over all beneath us. With our instructors peering down on us, tracking each person that we stepped on or even worse eliminated.

Peering into the assistance they supply us and the machinations that are performed on our behalf is important. It is vital to recognize that standing behind us isn't an empty space. We are not alone in our daily battle with life; there is an army of workers ready to answer our sincere calls and prayers.

We have an audience anxiously tracking our every movement. Analyzing what we did right and where and why we failed. An audience who cares and loves us, who don't wish to see the huge crash or pyrotechnics, for that, would constitute failure. The excitement lies in our gaining spiritual astuteness. They hope to discern signs that we are learning to balance our materialistic desires with our spiritual needs.

# Chapter 6 - Understanding Reincarnation

Many religions and individuals believe in reincarnation, but why does Spiritism believe in it? Spiritism contends that the early Christians also professed knowledge about our souls reincarnating, but this belief dissipated over the centuries after Christ. Spiritism renews the teachings of Christ and supplements them with the revelations promised to us.

If one looks at the vast literature written about reincarnation, covering our past lives, childhood memories of past lives, hypnosis revealing that some people lived on other planets, there seems to be many disjointed facets. While in truth, all are correct and all are similar according to the Doctrine of Spiritism. To understand the sweeping field of literature out in the world today, one should review the concept of reincarnation presented by Spiritism, and then all becomes clear. Spiritism provides the context, the rules, the process and the endgame for our multiple lives.

## Reincarnation

The Doctrine of Spiritism maintains that the goal of God and Jesus for us is for all of their children to become pure spirits. Each of us, through our own efforts, slowly advances toward the perfection of God. We will never reach the goal of absolute perfection, but we should come as close to pure love and harmony within the universe as possible. We are all immortal spirits; therefore we have until the end of time for our journey.

An example of a pure spirit is Jesus. One who truly loves us with all of his fiber, who understands the trials we must endure, our failings, our weaknesses, our petty jealousies, yet even still radiantly smiles down upon us, knowing that someday we shall become wholly integrated within the loving universe and take our places as a force for good.

The central question is; how do we become pure? The answer

lies within *The Spirits Book*:

*166. How can the soul that has not attained to perfection during the corporeal life complete the work of purification?*

"By undergoing the trial of a new existence"

*How does the soul accomplish this new existence? Is it through it transformation as a spirit?*

"The soul, in purifying itself, undoubtedly undergoes a transformation; but, in order to effect this transformation, it needs the trial of corporeal life"

*The soul has then, many corporeal existences?*

"Yes; we all have many such existences. Those who maintain the contrary wish to keep you in the same ignorance in which they are themselves."

*It would seem to results from this statement that the soul, after having quitted one body, takes another one; in other words, that it reincarnates itself in a new body. Is it thus that this statement is to be understood?*

"Evidently so."[29]

Therefore, to ascend we must accept the task of being reborn in a physical body. There are lessons that only can be learned through a bodily existence. But why do we need to reincarnate multiple times?

## The Need for Multiple Lives

Multiple lives are required, because one life doesn't supply the lessons required for us to ascend. The spirit Andre Luiz, who wrote many books, which were psychographed by Francisco C. Xavier, goes into great depth about various aspects of the spirit realm. In one book, he explores the need for us to be reborn over and over again. Andre Luiz was assigned to a group of spirits who assisted people leaving their earthly life in the book, *Workers of the Life*

*Eternal*, where he underwent numerous experiences at people's bedsides and witnessed the dramas that swirled around them. He weighs the frequent scenes and stories of people struggling to depart and comes to the conclusion:

> "Studying cases of death had enriched my knowledge in the field of mental science. The spirit, (eternal in essence) makes use of matter (transitory in its associations) as didactic material that evolves more and more in the spirit's never ending course of experience toward integration within the Supreme Divinity."[30]

What does Andre mean by didactic material in this instance? One of the definitions of didactic is "Teaching or intended to teach a moral lesson."[31] Therefore as we continue learning in the Spirit world and travel through various physical trials on earth we accumulate moral lessons that in turn influence our physical bodies and the structure of our brain, as we are reborn. Not only is our intellectual being as Spirits is important, but the physical makeup of our human form is vital for our involvement on our planet and to our eventual elevation as Spirits.

Given all that he had seen, Andre fully realizes the need for our multiple attempts at learning in our corporeal bodies, "Hence the reasons for the complex activities of the evolutionary road, the countless diversities, the multiplicity of social positions, the degrees of abilities and the levels of intelligence on the various planes of life."[32] What a wonderful revelation! We all go through periods of high social positions, living life with riches, and being the smartest person in the room. Although, we also live in the opposite positions. Truly, this knowledge must cause us all to be humble.

Being trapped in a material body affords us the opportunity to learn what is not possible to apprehend in the spirit world. While certainly, one can gather intellectual knowledge, the building of our emotions, of faith, charity, honor and love are rooted in the pain and suffering we are exposed to in the physical world. The Spirits Book backs up this thesis, in the secondary question to question 175:

- *Would it not be happier to remain as a spirit?*

"No, no! For we should remain stationary; and we want to advance towards God."[33]

For those who believe we only need one physical life to be pure, it is as if we wanted to be the President of a large company without ever working any other job. Of course we must start in the mail room and work our way up in various positions to fully comprehend how things get done and how to survive within the culture of the organization. No matter how pious we could have started out as a new spirit, we would still need the required know-how to gain our elevation. Only through rigorous trials do we have the right mixture of beliefs and knowledge to reincarnate with good prospects of success and to be a valued worker in the Spirit realm.

## Multiple Lives – Where?

Hence, we do need to accumulate a mountain of instances and encounters from all social, cultural, and physical environments. We are on task to build a strong foundation, upon which we can amass ever more knowledge and possess the wisdom to utilize it appropriately. So where do we begin to lay the base for our future? The answer, once again, lies in *The Spirits Book*:

*172. Do we accomplish all our different corporeal existences upon this earth?*

"Not all of them, for those existences take place in many different worlds. The world in which you now are is neither the first nor the last of these, but is one of those that are the most material, and the furthest removed from perfection."

*173. Does the soul, at each new corporeal existence pass from one world to another or can it accomplish several existences on the same globe?*

"It may live many times on the same globe, if it be not sufficiently advanced to pass into a higher one."

49

*We may, then, re-appear several times upon the earth?*

"Certainly."

*Can we come back to it after having lived in other worlds?"*

"Assuredly you can; you may already have lived elsewhere as upon the earth."[34]

The answers imply that we live on whatever worlds that we are required to do so, in order to gather the required curriculum. We are all interstellar travelers, but alas, our memories of our journeys are hidden from most of us. We regain those thoughts and remembrances when we return to the spirit world.

## Where are we heading?

Where does all of this lead to? Are we locked into paying for our wrongs and learning lessons the hard way forever? No, for at some time in our future existence, we will have built a wall of experiences that enable us to gather more knowledge and retain our humbleness and capacity to love, without any urge to act superior. Our next step is to be promoted to a world of regeneration.

The worlds of regeneration are described in Allan Kardec's, The Gospel According to Spiritism":

"Regenerative worlds serve as a transition between worlds of expiation and worlds of bliss. The repentant soul finds peace and repose on them, and ends up purifying itself. Of course, on such worlds humans are still subject to the laws that govern matter; their humanity still experiences your sensations and desires but is free of the muddled passions that enslave you; on regenerative worlds there is no longer the pride that renders your heart silent, the envy that tortures it and the hatred that suffocates it. The word love is written on every brow, a perfect equity governs social relationships, and all acknowledge God, endeavoring to evolve toward him by following his laws."[35]

Regenerative worlds are but one stop, there are more advance worlds that await us as we climb up the ladder to perfection. Most certainly, the description of a regenerative world is one of an earthly paradise to us. Where, while we still must reincarnate, our lives are not as brutish, full of drama that tears away at our quest to live serenely. A world where one can be happy and free to focus on the education that we agreed to before being reborn.

As one can see, there is no shortcut. No payment can be made to the right person to skip our trials. After all, a child can't become an adult in an instant, even though that child may be an extraordinary genius, the child must still grow emotionally so they could focus their intellectual energies at the right target. To all of us here, reading, at this very moment, we are all the same. The variations that we perceive to be so great are but minuscule to the spirit world. We are but a mass of unruly students, learning how to behave in an adult's world.

# Chapter 7 – Reincarnation Solves the Problem of Evil

In the last chapter we have established the concept that reincarnation is required. That only by living in the physical world can we transform ourselves into refined beings. So how does each birth slowly mold us?

Leon Denis, in his book, *Life and Destiny*, supplies the central tenet for the purpose of reincarnation:

"It explains the inequalities of human conditions, tastes, faculties, and characters. It dissipates the mysteries and contradictions of life. It solves the problems of evil."[36]

Knowing the earth is a planet of atonement, where spirits reincarnate to understand and correct their errors, clearly illustrates why there is such inhumanity among us. Spirits who have lived their previous lives on a primitive planet can't be expected to behave in a civilized manner, they must suffer through many trials here to comprehend the need for honor, love and charity.

Leon describes the reincarnation process, "Through it, order succeeds disorder, light comes from the bosom of chaos - injustice disappears, apparent iniquities of fate vanish, to give way to the majestic law of repercussion, of acts and consequences."[37]

We are put on the assembly line, so to speak, or more descriptive, a series of filters, where each successive filter, removes one more impurity. We advance one more step toward purity. Leon tells us the results:

"The doctrine of reincarnation brings men more closely together than any other belief in teaching them their common origin and end, and showing them the solidarity which unites them in the past, present, and future, it tells them there are no favorites, but each being is the son of his own works, the master of his own destiny." [38]

Hence, the criminal you see lurking on the street corner, waiting for their next victim, will one day be more like you. As you were similar to them in your past life. The reprobate that you scorn, may one day be a great missionary of faith. The wheels of reincarnation churn on and on, always crushing that bad instinct, the urge to take what you want, all dishonorable thoughts that now pollute our minds.

Eventually, each one of us will rise out of this muck, this bastion of evil, into a far better world, a regenerative world, where good outweighs evil and we are allowed to improve ourselves in a safer, more secure environment. Where we will learn more lessons; lessons that will open our eyes to worlds that we can't imagine today.

# Chapter 8 - What Does Immortality Mean?

Now we realize that we reincarnate as many times as it takes to remove all impurities, all blemishes, and all bad habits. That we are immortal spirits with an eternity to accomplish our goal. But, what does immortal really mean? It's like the concept of a very large number, we grasp the concept of the number, but we don't understand the enormity, the underlying meaning of the vastness of the numeral.

We hear the word immortality and immediately think, "We can live forever!" But how long and what is forever. This subject was discussed in the book, *Memoirs of a Suicide*, by Yvonne A. Pereira. A high-level spirit tells us what immortality means.

Yvonne A. Pereira, psychographed the book, Memoirs of a Suicide, published in 1955, with the help of two spirits, the first is Camilo Candido Botelho (his real name is Camilo Castelo Branco), a Portuguese writer who committed suicide on June 1, 1890. He wrote 58 books and was known as the Portuguese Balzac[39]. His eyesight was failing and he decided he didn't want to live any longer without sight. The other Spirit is Leon Denis, who was one of the leading apostles of Spiritism after the passing of Allan Kardec[40]. Leon Denis died in 1927. In Yvonne's preface, she mentions she has been writing the book since 1926, in communication with the deceased suicide, Camilo. Therefore, Leon Denis, who had died in 1927 was put to work rather rapidly to assist Yvonne to organize and edit her work. Already I have explained one aspect of immortality to you, there is always is time to work!

The spirit author, Camilo spent some time in the lower zones, a very unpleasant episode, and when his intended life span completed, he was picked up and taken to the Mary of Nazareth Hospital. The entire complex was controlled by the mother of Jesus and was dedicated to suicides. Camilo endured a lengthy process to recover from his desperate act. As part of his recovery he and the group he was recovering with, was able to speak with knowledgeable spirits about the various aspects of their life. This learned instructor told the assembled group:

"O humankind! Creatures forged from the radiant breath of the Divine Focal Point! Remember that you are immortal! … Ponder everything you see, touch and possess; the achievements that promote pride within you; the vanities that flatter your selfishness; the mad passions that debase your character and compromise your future; the fictitious worldly glories that cajole your conceit, enslaving you to materiality. All of this is doomed to pass away, to vanish one day, destroyed by the implacable fires of reality and submerged in the forgetfulness of untenable things that cannot last in the bosom of a Perfect Creation"[41]

Well, that exactly covered my dreams and aspirations! One more reason to rent instead of owning a home. We live our lives thinking of the weekend to come, next month when we get our bonus, of the joy when we pick up a new car, all for what? The excitement of a moment or one more toy to add to our stable. All will degrade into dust and we are the only trace left. Our immortal spirit, our aura of energy will still exist, while whatever possessions we attempted to accumulate throughout the eons are left like stranded vessels.

Wait, it gets better. The lecturer is just warming up, he has only reminded us of the futility of keepsakes, of cherishing anything but our own spirit and our capacity to love and be charitable to others.

"Remember the Sun, which has seen you being born and reborn so many times in the earth, giving you life, guiding and warming your steps, smiling at your victories as a progressing spirit, watching over your health and protecting you throughout the millennia, and collaborating with you in the struggles necessary for your education as a divine heir. All of them, too, shall pass away and die, to be replaced by new and better versions, which in turn will undergo the same fate! You, however, shall never pass away! You shall behold the

55

succession of the eons, like the One who created you and made you eternal like himself, endowing you with the essence of the life that comes from Him, and from whose bosom you have come forth!"[42]

We shall outlive the Sun and all of its successors. I believe that quite a few of us have thought about living as long as the sun, which according to "Wikipedia" will last another five billion years, after which it will turn into a red giant. My thoughts of infinite life has always revolved around my own planet. But, we shall all see earth grow cold and die one day, the entire solar system turn into a giant freezer. What happens then? What planet will we be sent to?

One day the total energy of the universe shall also be totally expended. Will we outlive this universe and one day be transferred to another? Being immortal is certainly giving me more questions than answers. The lecturer closes with these words of wisdom:

"Therefore, take heed, O Humankind! Because your rights of filiation have destined you for divine glory in the bosom of Eternity, you cannot evade the effort required of you for your evolution, the ascension that is proper to your very nature, so that you may reach the realm from which you descended! ... On that long, imperative road ahead of you, the more you infringe the principles that determine the harmonious scale of your ascent, the more you will suffer the effects of the dissonance you have created by breaking the Law you are subject to as a creature of a Perfect Being!"[43]

Hence, we all know the course of our life, it is one of eternal learning, with hopefully plenty of interludes of amusement and wonderment about the multitude variations that present themselves to us in this universe. While we may occasionally veer off-course, be thankful that you shall have plenty of time for the make-up classes.

# Chapter 9 – You have a Unique ID

A favorite saying is that "we are all unique". Sounds like an empty expression that is supposed to make us feel good about ourselves. But according to the Spirit world, we really are unique; we each have a radiation signature that is not the same as anyone else in the universe.

How else can we be tracked and analyzed? If we are to live through numerous births and deaths, then there must be some method to identify us in whatever body we may reside.

In the books dictated to Francisco C. Xavier, by the spirit author Andre Luiz, there are always nuggets of startling new information. As soon as I started reading *In the Realms of Mediumship*, published in 1955, I noticed an unusual introduction by the spirit Emmanuel, who usually writes moral exhortations. He began the introduction, titled, "Rays, Waves, Mediums, Minds…" by surveying the history of science in what makes up our universe. He started with Leucippus, about 500 years before Christ, who theorized that everything was composed of atoms. Surveying others, including the Curies, who discovered radium. Finally mentioning Bohrs, Planck, and Einstein, where he writes:

"The vehicle of flesh, the human body, is now nothing more than an electric vortex governed by consciousness.

Each tangible body is a bundle of concentrated energy. Matter is transformed into energy, and energy disappears to give way to matter.

Raised to the status of investigators of the truth, chemist and physicists, geometricians and mathematicians have become today's priest of the spirit without desiring it. Due to their ongoing studies, materialism and atheism will be compelled to vanish for lack of matter, the base that had ensured their negativistic speculations.

Laboratories are temples in which intelligence is driven to serve God; and even when intellectual activity is misguided, temporarily subordinated to the political hegemony that generates wars, the progress of science as a divine conquest continues to exalt the good and is bound for a glorious future.

That future belongs to the spirit!"[44]

I believe he is telling us, that no matter what a scientist believes as regards to a higher power, he or she is working toward the day, when the existence of the spirit world can't be doubted. Which, even *The Spirits Book*, by Allan Kardec, tells us will occur one day. Now for the new information:

"Through the sentiments that characterize their inner life, all individuals emit specific rays and live within the spiritual wave with which they identify themselves.

Such truths cannot remain semi-hidden in our sanctuaries of faith; they will radiate from the temples of science like mathematical equations."[45]

Hence we all have a unique identification, the same as a RFID (Radio Frequency Identification) chip, which is used to track packages and even help you check out goods from a store. It is a chip with a low level energy transmitter that is attached to each individual good so computer systems will instantly know the location, price, and description of the object.

### What Does This Mean to Us?

In many religious books, there are always stories of people having their prayers answered. Have you ever wondered how does the spirit world discern our prayers and calls for help amongst the enormous background noise of billions of thoughts emanating from humans every minute? The same principle of the internet, where each message you transmit from your laptop, iPad, or cell phone, has your unique, in the entire world, IP (Internet Protocol) address, which shows, to the knowledgeable, your country of origin, the time sent and even the operating system software you are using to send the message. Therefore, our every thought must be tagged with our spirit ID!

As our brain is active, thinking and sending out its transmissions, there is an immense facility out in the universe gathering, categorizing, and analyzing the information received. Hence, by the virtue of having our individual spiritual wave, we are instantly recognized, no matter what the circumstances are, by the spirit world. In other words, God is always watching us.

Not only Emmanuel tells us, but a lecturer, Instructor Alberio, at the Ministry of Communications at Nossa Lar, explains to us:

"So, we comprise a vast group of intelligences that are attuned to the same vibratory pattern of perception. We are part of a Whole made up of billions of being that form, so to speak earthly humankind.

Thus, as only a humble family in the infinite concert of cosmic life, in which each world harbors only one specific family of Universal Humanity, we know for the time being merely those expressions of life that most closely speak to us, limited as we are in the degree of knowledge we have acquired so far."[46]

Therefore, we humans are a separate branch of the Universal Humanity; we have our own class of emanating wavelengths. If we reincarnate on another world, our appearance may change, our pattern of radiation may alter slightly, but we always retain our spirit ID.

## The Psychoscope

Since we all radiate a unique signature, it seems reasonable that a device could be created to read our signature and the state of our mind. The spirit world has a device and it is called a Psychoscope. Aulus, who the is person taking Andre Luiz and his companion Hilario to visit a Spiritual center, describes the device:

"It's an apparatus that an illustrious student of spirit phenomenology intuitively referred to at the end of the last century. It's design to probe the soul. It has the power to define the soul's vibrations and the ability to make diverse observations regarding the subject." Aulus explained with a smile. "We hope that in the future it will be available to human beings. It runs on electricity and magnetism, utilizing radiant elements similar in essence to gamma rays. It is composed of lenses for observation that can also be used for microphotography."[47]

Andre asks if the Psychoscope can be used on spirits; Aulus replies:

"Certainly," Aulus answered good-naturedly. "We are all subject to being probed by the higher planes, just as we currently investigate the planes situated below ours. If the spectroscope enables a person to investigate the nature of the chemical elements found at enormous distances by analyzing the light waves they emit, we can much more easily discern the qualities of a person by the rays he or she emits. Morality, sentiments, education and character are clearly discernible through a brief inspection."[48]

Get ready for the day when we are all an open book. Nothing is hidden from the psychoscope. If you want to rent an apartment, first you must pass the psychoscope. Want a job? Well, step up and present yourself to the psychoscope. Sounds frightening? Only because we are worried about our own flawed behavior.

The spirit world, where they live everyday banded together by the Law of Affinity, where like-minded spirits are attracted to each other, already live in system of constant selection based upon their character. We, on the other hand, may congregate in housing projects, exclusive cities, or slums as the case may be, but for most of our waking day we exist in a mass of people who constantly think honest, dis-honest and all flavors in-between thoughts.

The spirit world sees the positive possibilities:

"The psychoscope itself is a motive for important considerations. Just think of a human society that could expose the inner life of its members! It would save an enormous amount of time in the solution of numerous psychological problems."[49]

Yes, it could be wonderful for certain situations, but how will people in power use this device? I can only hope that by the time it is invented on earth, we have advanced enough to use it wisely.

## What Does the Psychoscope Show?

What does one see when looking through the scope? Andre Luiz has a try and here is what he perceives:

"Without any mental effort, I noticed that all the expressions of physical matter took on a different appearance, especially the matter from our place.

The roof, the walls, and other commonplace objects revealed themselves to be formed of currents of energy emitting a hazy glow.

I turned around to contemplate the incarnates. They now appeared to be more closely associated with one another by means of broad radiant circles that hovered over their heads in opal-like splendor.

I had the impression of seeing a corona of solar light around the opaque block of semi-dark mass to which the table had been reduced. The corona was comprised of ten individual points. The center of each one of them projected the spiritual faces of the praying incarnates.

From that chain of golden focal points, a wide band of violet light extended outward. This band appeared to be contained within another band of orangey light overflowing in diverse tones, which I couldn't identify, because my attention was fixed on the circle of illuminated faces visibly united like ten tiny suns all connected to each other. I noticed that above each of them was a halo of nearly-vertical shiny, moving beams of light that looked like small antennae of smoldering gold. These halos differed from one incarnated to the next, and abundant clusters of stellar luminosity fell on each from On High. When they touched the heads of those gathered there, they seemed like soft currents of energy that turned into microscopic petals that flickered with light and then went out in myriads of delicate and whimsical forms, gravitating momentarily around the brains where they were produced, like short-lived satellites swirling around the vital forms from which they emanated.

Spirit mentors guarded the assembly, each one radiating his or her own light."[50]

Each of us a transmitting tower and a receiving station, where information is passed back and forth in constant motion, all deciphered by our active brain and perispirit. Aulus tells Andre and Hilario, "Don't you know that an incarnate individual is a generator of electromagnetic power, with one oscillation per second registered by the heart? Are you by chance unaware of the fact that all living substances on earth emit energies, framed in the bands of ultraviolet radiations?"[51] Hence, we are always on, always participating in a world around us, that we can't see or touch, but our soul knows, understands, and acts on these messages.

Aulus then goes on to explain "vital rays", which are mental rays that are projected and received and play an important part in our life. Aulus states, "All individual have them, however, and emit them at a frequency that varies with each individual, according to the tasks that their Life Plan has assigned to them."[52]

In addition to our spirit ID, we have our time code. A code that denotes the stage of our Life Plan that we are currently in and maybe even transmitting the grade we are receiving for our performance.

I apologize for the scope of this chapter, it started out that we are all unique individuals and you were probably expecting a homily on how wonderful we all are. Instead, you have been presented with the specter of all of us being completely exposed, tracked, graded, and analyzed in a minute by minute basis. Plus, the promise of a future where even other humans will be able to see right through us. A bit daunting, yes. But, at least you know and now have the opportunity to internalize the significance of learning to become a better person. For there is no alternative, only longer periods of training, to our quest to grow into pure spirits.

# Chapter 10 - When you sleep you are Being Assisted

The spirit world fully realizes our vulnerabilities and absolute worthlessness of most of our daily thoughts. Transforming our actions, attitudes and inner most contemplations is a demanding exercise, which would be almost impossible to accomplish by ourselves. Therefore, help is constantly at our door.

In the book, *In the Greater World*, by the spirit Andre Luiz and psychographed by Francisco C. Xavier, Andre Luiz documents some of the assistance which is provided for people who are trying to learn and evangelize Spiritism. This is only an example, for there are other lectures and assistance given to those who are on their exploration for greater spiritual knowledge.

Once a person discovers Spiritism, the breadth of its doctrines soon become clear. Instead of a casual relationship one has with going to a local place of worship, where you are able to mediate and recharge your spiritual batteries on a once a week basis, the knowledge that every action we take is judged, that we are surrounded by other spirits, that we have a duty to spread love and our awareness, can make our discovery seem, at times, a heavy burden. The Spirit world recognizes the difficulties of balancing our spiritual lives while living in a materialistically dominated world. Andre Luiz, in the book, *In the Greater World*, is told about the assistance given to Spiritists:

"Through their diligent efforts in spiritualizing work, they are the future instruments for the endeavors that lie ahead. In spite of the clarity of the rules they live by, they still suffer disharmony and afflictions that threaten their incipient stability. Even so, they aren't left without the assistance they need. In our spheres of action, institutions for restoring their energies open their welcoming doors to them. Freedom from the body during sleep is the direct resource of our manifestations of fraternal support. At first, they receive our influence unconsciously; then their minds are slowly strengthened and they begin recording our concourse in their memory as we give them ideas, suggestions and opinions along with beneficial and redeeming inspirations by means of imprecise recollections."[53]

Andre Luiz is introduced to one such method of aid. His instructor takes him to a lecture given by the spirit Eusebio. Instructor Eusebio presents a lecture to those incarnated souls who have the desire for learning more and becoming active Spiritists, but are daily facing the obstacles we all encounter and still have that element of doubt in the absolute reality of our immortal soul. Andre is told that every person who is able to promote Spiritism is vital. The importance of the training is explained by Andre's companion, "Chance doesn't perform miracles. Any undertaking requires planning, execution and completion. The miracle of changing a physical person into a spiritual person requires a lot of collaboration on our part."[54]

## The Lecture for Spiritists

Eusebio begins the lecture by clarifying how his talk will affect each individual at the meeting, "Of course, because the deficiencies of the brain render it incapable of supporting the burden of two lives at the same time, you will not retain a full recollection of this hour upon reentering the corporeal envelope. Nevertheless, the memory of our meeting here will linger in the depths of your being, guiding your higher inclinations toward lofty purposes and opening your intuitive portal so that our fraternal thoughts may assist you."[55]

Eusebio explains to his audience how humanity has arrived at this precise moment. He recounts the sacred reading of the Old Testament by the Jews, who then would go out and fight the Philistines, the reverential praise of the writings of Marcus Aurelius, while the same his Roman government ordered the murder of innocents. He closes his point with, "In such a state we have reached the modern era, in which madness is widespread and men and women's mental stability is on the verge of disaster. With an evolved brain and an immature heart, we hone our art of wrecking our spiritual progress."[56]

Stressing the significance of maintaining our energy and increasing our self-enlightenment, Eusebio acknowledges the importance of such activities. But, as his warms to his subject, he notifies his listeners that individuals who strive to focus on themselves in their quest for purification is not good enough. He throws out the challenge, "If you wish to be pioneers of the living faith in the world, from now on, in spite of the difficulties, a complete demonstration of your convictions of divine spirituality will be required of you."[57]

At this point Eusebio reveals the mission, "Modern spiritualism cannot confine God within the walls of an earthly temple, for our essential mission is to change the whole earth into the majestic temple of God."[58] Eusebio is telling us that adding a Spiritual center next to the local church or temple, for those select few that will take the time to drop in, is totally inadequate. Our job is to change the world. Change from a materialistic centered society to a balanced one. Where, yes, scientific advancement is encouraged, new goods can be developed, but where the culture understands the importance of fraternal love and that all actions have a consequence. Where each individual recognizes they have past penalties to pay and they have mostly themselves to look toward to paying off their debts.

After the call to change the world, comes the command to organize ourselves for the task, "For our vanguard of determined and brave workers, the phase of futile experimentation, disorderly investigation and peripheral reasoning has passed."[59] We are being asked actively evangelize the doctrine of Spiritism. Set up gatherings to bring people into the fold and to seek out ways to publicize our message to others so they may, at the least, have the option to be exposed to the truth.

The importance of this is stated in Allan Kardec's *Genesis*, where the future of Spiritism and the transformation of the earth to a higher status is heralded by the gradual transition of more spirits which will be reincarnated with a *propensity for the good*.[60] For the good spirits amongst us, they need to hear our message, because these spirits will be, according to *Genesis*, "Charged with the founding the age of moral progress, the new generation is distinguishable by an overall precocious intelligence and reason combined with an *innate* sentiment of the good and spiritual beliefs – an unmistakable sign of a certain degree of *previous* advancement."[61] Focus on the word *innate*, meaning in this instance, "Coming directly from the mind".[62] An external trigger must exist for this feeling to come to the surface and be acted upon.

This task will not be without difficulty, pain or sacrifice. Eusebio puts our efforts in context, "Jesus did not reach the culmination of resurrection without climbing Calvary, and his lessons refer to the faith that moves mountains".[63] Next, to emphasize his point, Eusebio throws out a litany of advice to surmount the impediments:

"Do not go looking for miracles: yearning for them can become addictive and lead to your loss."

"Your burdens on the earthly landscape, however rough or displeasing, represent the Supreme Will."

"Do not jump over obstacles or try to go around them in a deliberate attempt to escape: conquer them using will and perseverance, providing an opportunity to develop your growth."[64]

As well as supplying the reason, the method and the hurdles of promoting Spiritism, Eusebio lays out the context of our struggle in today's environment, "The powerful winds of the evolutionary wave are sweeping the earth. Every day we see the collapse of conventional principles held inviolable for centuries. The perplexed human mind is forced to make distressful changes. The subversion of values, the social experiment and the accelerated process of selection through collective suffering perturb the timid and inattentive, who represent the overwhelming majority everywhere." [65]

The lecture given by Eusebio was not a homily filled discourse on how we can grow as a Spiritist. This was a, "get out of your chair and do something about it", speech. A call to arms, where we are told the objective, the terrain, and the difficulties that we should expect on the way. If it wasn't clear before, it should be clear now, being a Spiritist is not an easy task.

## The Lecture for Catholics and Protestants

Now, let's contrast the speech given to Spiritists with a lecture delivered to a group of incarnate Catholics and Protestants. Later in the book, *In the Greater World*, Andre Luiz is invited to hear a lecture, again by Eusebio, to a mixed group of Catholics and Protestant, albeit a less dogmatic and more likely to be persuaded types of persons. Andre Luiz was surprised that the lecture was being held, he was told, "It's important to understand that Divine Protection shows no privileges. Heavenly grace is like the fruit that always results from earthly effort: wherever there is human cooperation, there too will be Divine support."[66] This information leads us to believe the tone and substance of lecture will be similar. A call to action, a request to get with the program.

As in the first lecture, Eusebio opens with what it meant to be a Christian in ancient times and reviewed the sacrifices they underwent. Next, Eusebio offers a challenge, "However, as heir to those nameless heroes who lived in affliction, of minds built up in the promises of Christ, what have you done with transforming hope, with unwavering trust? What have you done with the living faith that your forbearers acquired at the price of blood and tears?"[67]

Eusebio then delves into his opinion of exactly what these institutions of faith have actually accomplished:

"You have erected barriers against each other that are difficult to cross. Dogmatism poisons you; schism corrupts you. Narrow interpretations of the divine plan darken your mental horizons."

"What delirium has taken you as you involve yourselves in a mutual competition for the imaginary obtainment of divine privileges?"

"In times of old, Christ's disciples competed for opportunities to serve, whereas today, you look for every little opportunity to be served."[68]

After a devastating review of their faults, Eusebio arrives at his request, "Therefore, do not limit your demonstration of trust in the Most High to the ceremonies of outward worship. Get rid of the indifference that chills your ornate cathedrals. Let us make ourselves each other's true brothers and sisters. Let is transform the church into the sweet home of the Christian family, whatever our interpretations might be."[69] This is it? A plea for a less bureaucratic and more involved practice of their religious principles, and an appeal for less infighting and more focus on the fraternal family under Christ?

Whereas, the goal for Spiritists is the change the world, the request for the souls at the lecture is to return to their Christian roots and stop fighting each other. The Spirit world is not expecting the audience to change the world, but to outwardly demonstrate the teaching of Christ as revealed in the New Testament. The Spirit world is first attempting to steer the ship of the large religious organizations back onto a truly fraternal course. Without this correction, the ability and the required openness to accept the Spiritist doctrine would be absent.

## Time to Wake-up

As if you didn't need more work in your life, you now have your second (or third or fourth for some) job. But remember the reward, a happier planet, a place where strife and the constant jockeying for position in even the smallest things is unknown. Not a steep price to pay for an immortal soul with plenty of time to live the good and a contented productive life in the future.

# Chapter 11 – Higher Spirits Who Come to Help Us

As part of the process to guide us poor souls stuck on this planet, a core group of high spirits must lead the charge. For they are the visible manifestation of God's will that we shall progress. Without leadership from those who supply the ideal behavior and a code of ethics that we must strive to adhere, the rest of us would struggle to find our direction.

Who are the higher spirits that come to earth to help our planet progress? Why would they consent to live through pain and suffering to assist so many ungrateful souls? Leon Denis in his book, *Life and Destiny*, tells us who are these selfless spirits and the reason for their voluntary descent into our environment of pain and atonement.

Leon recounts what these superior spirits withstood on their climb toward perfection:

"To construct an individuality, through thousands of lives, accomplished in hundreds of worlds, and under the direction of our older brothers and our friends in space, to climb the paths to Heaven, to the divine drama, one of the agents of God in the eternal work; to work for the universe as the universe works for us, behold the secret of destiny! So the soul mounts from sphere to sphere, from circle to circle. United to the beings it has loved, it goes on its pilgrimage, seeking divine perfection. Arriving at the supreme region, it is freed from the law of rebirth. Reincarnation is no more an obligation for it, but an act of will, and a work of sacrifice when it has a mission to accomplish. Reaching the supreme height, the spirit says: "I am free! I have broken forever the fetters which has chained me to material worlds; I have acquired science, energy, love. But that which I have acquired I want to share with my brothers, and for that purpose I will go and live among them, and I will offer them the best that is in me. I will take a body of flesh, I will descend again among those who suffer in ignorance, to console, enlighten and aid."[70]

The thorny path to perfection is long and arduous. We who are here now are just beginning our education. Imagine what we will learn in the future? The span of humanity and the vast discoveries to be witnessed. Would we have the love to return to the abyss and help others? I would think that after we truly learn to rid ourselves of our ego, our desire for material possessions that anyone of us could someday be what Leon Denis says are high spirits that have lowered themselves to aid us, "And then we have Lao-tsze, Buddha, Socrates, Christ."[71]

An impressive list of spirits that left a legacy of good in their wake. These are the models that we shall one day follow. Not now, or in the distant future for most of us, but think of eternity, over the course of a million years and countless lives. As we mend our defects step by step, imagine a perfect you. Someday it shall happen.

# Chapter 12 – How Spirits Help and Guide Us

With the example of Christ and his divine messengers, who have journeyed to earth over the course of centuries to grant us role models and codes of behavior that we should strive to emulate, also comes an army of spirits to assist humankind. Spirits who have ascended in their multiple lives, but aren't on the level of higher spirits, who, nevertheless desire to take part in the evolution of earth and its people. The spirit world understands having a book available to refer to find the desired conduct is simply not sufficient for our distracted and anxious brains. An infantry of aides, feet on the ground, is indispensable for our eventual victory.

The most important point to realize as we travel toward our current destiny is that we are not on this journey alone. The spirit world is concerned with each and every one of us. Our guardian angels take no pleasure seeing us struggle, since they have all been there before. Even though, they comprehend that most times we need the suffering presented to us. But within the confines of letting us survive and learn from our trials, the spirit world actively guides and helps us.

During and after birth we are looked after by the spirit world. In the book, *Missionaries of the Light*, another Andre Luiz inspired book, psychographed by Chico Xavier, we are told of the constant care we receive after birth:

> "Friends, Herculano will remain at Segismundo's side for seven years in his new reincarnation, at which time the reincarnation process will have been completed. After that period, his work as a friend and guide will be eased, for he will follow our brother at a distance."[72]

The spirit Herculano, who assisted during the conception and birth of Segismundo, shall stay constantly at his side for seven years. Did you ever wonder how babies can seemly survive so many dangers in their young life? Or how when young toddlers walk, looking backwards or anywhere but in front of them, why don't they bump into more objects? Because they are influenced to avoid hazards by their spirit guardian.

As to the time period of seven years, that is explained to Andre Luiz by his mentor:

"You are aware that the human body has its vegetative activities per se, but you may not yet know that the perispiritual body, which gives form to the cellular elements, is strongly rooted in the blood. In the fetal organization, the blood elements are a gift from the mother's body. Soon after rebirth, a period of a different assimilation of organic energies takes place, where the reincarnated 'self' rehearses the consolidation of its new experiences. In this new cycle of physical life, it is only at age seven that it can begin to preside on its own over the blood formation process, which is the basic element for the equilibrium of the perispiritual body or pre-existent form. Blood, therefore, can be regarded as the divine fluid that underpins our activities on the physical plane, and through its continual flow within the physiological organism, it furnishes us with a symbol of the eternal movement of the sublime energies of the Infinite Creation."[73]

The process of reincarnation, even after birth, is complex. For our spirit body to be connected to our physical body via the perispirit is a seven year long process. Not only does the child have the full time attention of their mother and father, but the spirit world supplies an invisible sentry. Continuously protecting the young child. Life is more precious than we could ever imagine.

## How we are assisted as Adults

Not only children require support from the spirit world, we do too. Again, in the book, *Missionaries of the Light*, a young woman, with small children lost her husband and was inconsolable. To supply her closure with her dead husband, the spirit world arranged a visit with him, during her sleep, when she could leave the bounds of her body. She was able to talk to him and find out that he was safe in the spirit world.

Since, our spirits can communicate directly with other spirits during our slumber, we learn many valuable lessons and have various conversations with other spirits, spirits who could reside in the spirit world or other incarnates, who had left their body. We are unable to retain exact memories of these encounters. But we do awaken with general ideas and feelings. Just like the widow did from her sleep, when her aunt asked her if she actually believed she visited her husband in a dream the night before:

"Why not?" replied the widow without blinking, "I still have the feeling of his hands on mine, and I know that God granted me such grace so that I could find my strength again to work. Today I woke up totally refreshed and happy! I can face the future with new hope! I will make an effort and I shall be victorious."

"Oh Mommy, how your words console us!" exclaimed one of the little ones with bright eyes. "How I wish I could have been with you to listen to Daddy in that wonderful dream!" [74]

When you arise in the morning from a satisfying sleep and you feel good for no apparent reason, this could be a residue from a nocturnal encounter. Or when you leap out of bed ready to tackle that problem which had been bothering you for days, this could be the result of you finding out the solution while talking with your friends or guides in the spirit world.

If we search for the answer it will come. The spirit world wishes to supply us with all of the tools and inspirations required to prosper while we live on earth. They fully realize the day-to-day problems we come across, complications which hinder our ability to absorb the lessons we should learn. Therefore, like any good teacher, who wishes their students to be successful, the spirit world gently pushes us to the correct solution. We have to listen to our conscience, that governor of our behavior, with years of experience in many lives, and perform our deeds with moral clarity.

### Favors Returned

When we perform good deeds, the resulting wave of our

charity rolls back toward us. People who we have aided think caring thoughts about us, spirits who assist the ones we materially help also notice our benevolence. A good example of this is found in the book, *Action and Reaction*, a spirit, a young man who died and is now watching over his mother, asks for a favor:

"My dear Assistant, our Adelino is having financial problems ... Because he helps others so much, he has been neglecting his own needs. He is always helping my poor incarnate mother, so I would ask for your help on his behalf. Just last week, my widowed mother didn't have the means to get medical treatment for my two sick brothers, so I went to him in tears and mentally begged him to help us out. He didn't hesitate for a second. Believing he was obeying his own impulses, he visited our house and gave my poor mother the money she needed ... Dear Assistant! For the love of Jesus, I beg you! Don't forsake someone who has helped us out so much!"[75]

Sacrifices on our part for others, should be seen as opportunities to spread goodwill. The more goodwill we radiate, the more it will bounce back to us, enabling us to give even more. Doing well is not a zero sum game, I give and you take, no it's a positive feedback loop, with a rising crescendo of light and joy that shall surround us.

The young man is answered by the Assistant:

"Don't worry, Adelino is in a web of fraternal affinity that he has woven for himself. A lot of friends are supplying him with the resources he needs to faithfully carry out his caring task. Circumstances of a material nature will come together in his favor as a consequence of acquired merit."[76]

As you can ascertain, the little things that happen in our life, a coincidence here, a random event there that brings us unexpected joy, or the break to find a job that we always desired, could all be in response to the charity we have spread before. We are truly cared for by the spirit world. When we exhibit good behavior, our mentors wish to reward us to continue to do so.

Before we reincarnate, we realize that we have much ground to cover to become better souls. Each little victory is one step closer to achieving our level of purity.

## The Spirit World Knows our Grades

While it may seem that random conversations among spirits affect the level of assistance we receive, the truth is more revealing. Once again, our old concept of heaven as an Elysian field of bliss and comfort, must be replaced by processes that are all too familiar to us. Why should we expect heaven to be so different than on earth? Yes, everything is better and more alive with energy, but spirits are still the same after death. Once a person dies, they do not transform into a wise benevolent saint, no they are the same as before, with more intelligence and composed of different matter, but thinking along the same lines as always. Hence, the processes of watching over us and tracking our progress is the same as if we were in school.

In one of the specialized colonies in the spirit world, Almas Irmas (Spirit Sisters), they educate spirits and help them prepare for their next reincarnation. In the book, *Sex and Destiny*, another Andre Luiz inspired tome, Andre is told how the students who were reborn are followed:

"All reincarnate individualities connected with Almas Irmas have files containing the entire history of what they are accomplishing during their reincarnation. These files indicate not only the balance of the credits earned but also the debts acquired. This balance can be examined at any time so as to provide them with the help they deserve, depending on the loyalty they demonstrate in keeping the obligations they undertook and according to their willingness to contribute to the general good."[77]

Oh! That word "deserve", I always hated that growing up. Listening to my parents telling me that I didn't deserve something. I wanted to just get what I craved, without having to earn it. How unjust the world is! To my little mind, of course.

I am hardly better now, with my longing for objects or events that I have in no way served my time in earning them. We can't escape the fact that we must work for what we receive. This is the mundane secret of the heaven awaiting us. Processes, such as earning your living, don't disappear with death, they are just altered. Not to say, they aren't changed for the spectacularly better, where we work in our desired vocation, not just to survive. Nevertheless, we can't escape the concept of debit and credit.

Hence, to receive you must give, for as Jesus said it is always better to give than to receive, he knew what he was talking about. This wasn't just some remote ideal to make us better souls. It was practical advice on how to be successful in the spirit world.

## End of Life Assistance

For those of us that have accumulated a bounty of love along the path of our life, the spirit world lends us and our family a hand in our final passage. In the book, *Workers of the Life Eternal*, Andre Luiz is a member of a team that assist people to leave their physical bodies to return to life in the spirit world. The discarnated father of the old man dying with his family around him asks the other spirits to work with him to make his son's, Fabio, last hours pleasant. He asks the team:

> "I know that Fabio's liberation will require a great deal of effort. However, I would like to help him with the last home worship in which he will physically participate at his family's side. As a general rule, a dying person's last words are more affectionately recorded in the memory of those who remain behind. For that reason, I would really like to help him say a few words of advice and encouragement to his wife."[78]

The team of spirits applied length-wise passes over Fabio's whole body, giving him the strength to participate at his last family gathering. Fabio tells his wife that he will always love her and that she should find comfort with another if that is her wish. He tells her that he will help her all he can while in the spirit realm.

Fabio's father put his hand on Fabio's forehead and inspires

Fabio to say:

"I'm happy to have this opportunity to exchange ideas with you alone according to the faith we share. Significant is the absence of our old friends, who, for so many years, have accompanied us in our family prayers. There is a reason for that. We must talk about our needs, full of courage but never forgetting about the upcoming farewell. These words of the Apostle to the Gentiles are symbolic for our current situation. Just as there are mortal bodies, there are also spiritual bodies. And we can't ignore the fact that my mortal body will soon be returned to the welcoming earth, the common mother of the perishable forms in which we move about on the face of the globe. Something deep down tells me that this will perhaps be the last night that I will meet with you in this material body ... At times when sleep blesses me, I feel that I am on the verge of the great deliverance ... I can see that enlightened friends have been preparing my soul, and I am sure I will leave at the first opportunity. I believe all the necessary measures have already been taken to ensure our tranquility during these moments before the separation. In fact, I'm not leaving you any money but I find comfort in knowing that we have built the spiritual home of our sublime union, and it will be an indelible source of reference for our everlasting happiness ..."[79]

Fabio dies peacefully later that night, while his loving family is consoled and deeply touched by his last words. What better ending to a physical life than what Fabio and his spirit helpers were able to construct. He gave spiritual advice, joy, and hope in his final moments. There would be no need to second guessing from his family about the end. No regrets of not saying the final farewell.

For the last words are not about saying goodbye forever, but a message of see you soon. For at some point of time in the future, all shall be reunited in the real world, the domain of the spirits. The universe where we actually live the vast majority of time, for as we gain purity, we reincarnate less and less. Until, we come to the junction where to reincarnate is a choice, a mission gladly undertaken to help others as others have supported us before.

# Chapter 13 – Energizing Passes - How the Spirit World Restore our Balance

Not only does the spirit world support us in our endeavors, but they intervene when required to right our terrestrial body. In Spiritist Centers, passes are given to restore your well-being. For those who have earned the benefit, spirits will channel energy for each individual that desires divine assistance.

The transfer of energy from one being to another is the essence of a pass, as it is known in Spiritism. Passes revitalize our Vital Fluids so we may be stronger to face our daily trials. For if we don't place ourselves in a balanced state, we have less control over our emotions and our body is less able to heal itself.

### What are Passes

Passes are given in Spiritual Centers. The object of the Pass is to resupply your Vital Fluids to improve the harmony of your body, which should result in better physical and mental health.

Your body utilizes Vital Fluids, which is a modification of the Universal Fluids that make up everything in the Universe, these are altered to fit your own spirit and body. Vital Fluid can be thought as an energy force that maintains the various Force centers, otherwise known as Chakras, which are responsible for keeping all of your bodily functions in harmony. The more Vital Fluids you have, the healthier and more vitality you will possess.

A benefactor spirit transfers their fluids that they direct from Universal Fluids, into their own spirit. Next the benefactor spirit directs the flow to the physical person applying the passes. The person's perispirit and body transform the fluids from the spirit to Vital Fluids that conform to the patient's requirements. Thereby, customizing the form of energy to help the patient into the exact type of force they require. Below is a diagram of the process.

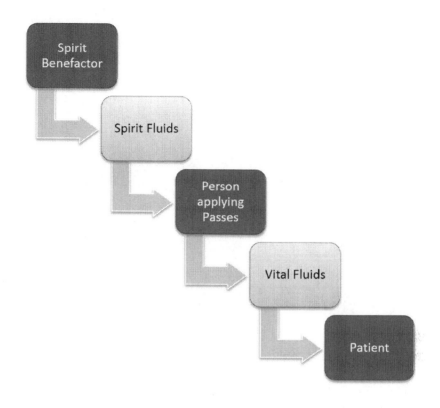

This transfer of Vital Fluids is done with the assistance of two beings. One is the loving and caring spirit who uses the physical person giving the passes as a channel to supply you with energy. The person giving the passes must be in harmony and full of goodwill toward their fellow beings. As the picture below illustrates, the spirit stands behind the pass giver who stands in front of you to deliver the vital fluids.

Passe espiritual:
Espírito - Médium - Assistido

I have received passes and I have definitely felt better. Could this just be all in my own mind and I wanted to feel restored? Yes, that could be one explanation, but with the other phenomena I have witnessed with Spiritism, I am a believer in ability of the spirit world to help us in every way possible so we may overcome our trials during our life.

## Why are Passes Given

As covered above, Passes are given to help a person recover their balance, the harmony of their spirit, perispirit and physical body.

Andre Luiz, our spiritual friend of many books, asks what are the benefits of passes and receives an answer from the spirit leader of the group giving passes to incarnates and discarnates:

"Just as the physical body can ingest poisonous foods that intoxicate its tissues, the perispiritual body can also absorb degenerative elements that corrode its energy centers with repercussions on the material cells. If an incarnate person's mind has not yet managed to discipline the emotions, if it nourishes passions that disharmonize it with reality, it can at any moment become poisoned with the mental emissions of those with whom it lives, and who are also in the same state of imbalance. Sometimes, these absorptions are simple phenomena of no major importance; however, in many cases they are susceptible of causing dangerous organic disasters. This happens particularly when the interested parties do not have a prayer life, the beneficial influence of which can annul many ills"[80]

The paragraph is eerily similar to my life before I discovered Spiritism. They could have replaced the word "person" with my name and been spot on. I wasn't been able to control my emotions, I was in a situation with no support and my life was completely absence of prayer or even the acknowledgment of the love of God and Jesus.

Hence, I was fat, well I am still overweight, but before even worse, had high blood pressure, headaches, and when I caught any illness it lingered for quite a while. Even though, I still get sick occasionally, when I do I recover quickly, my blood pressure is normal and my stress levels are very manageable. I can't remember my last headache.

Does my experience prove anything, no of course not, it could all be a coincidence. But since discovering Spiritism, I am less certain of anything that could be labelled a "coincidence". Once you come to the realization that we exist in a glass cage, where we go about our business blind to the presence of our mentors, you start to notice the small and large effects that push and pull you like the rolling waves in the middle of the ocean.

Let's see a pass in action and determine the benefits it gives you. There is a perfect example in the book, *Missionaries of the Light*, where Andre watches Anacleto manage the passes process. Andre asks if he could see a demonstration of the benefits of the procedure, and Anacleto points to a woman and tells him:

83

"This morning she had a bad argument with her husband and entered a serious state of inner disharmony. The small cloud surrounding her vital organ represents fulminating mental matter. The permanence of such residues in her heart could cause a dangerous illness. Let's help her."[81]

Andre then saw that Anacleto, with the help of an incarnate Spiritist, directed the energy of the Vital Fluids, in the form of a ray of light, toward the woman's heart. Andre describes the healing that he witness:

"Besieged by these magnetic principles, the small amount of black matter enveloping the mitral valve slowly moved away, and as if attracted by Anacleto's strong will, it reached the upper tissues, scattering under the radiating hand along the epidermis. Then the spirit magnetizer began the more active phase of the passes, discarding the evil influence. He made a double pass over the epigastric area by lifting both hands and immediately bringing them down very slowly past the hips down to the knees, repeating the same pass and operation over the area several times. In just a few moments the infirm woman's body returned to normal."[82]

Andre was amazed at the speed and completeness of the healing. Next he was curious to know, what would have happened to the woman, if she didn't visit a Spiritist Center. Would she be able to heal herself? Andre is told anyone who is living the religion that follows the path of the good will receive spiritual assistance, as long as they ask for help in prayer and trust in God. Anacleto goes on to describe where their assistance reaches:

"Whether she was praying in a Roman Catholic Church or in a Buddhist temple, she would receive help from our sphere by means of this or that group of Christ's worker. Of course, here in an organization that is free of the shadows of prejudice and dogma, our fraternal help can be more effective and purer, and the possibilities for her profiting are much greater. However, I need to point out that magnetic helpers go wherever there are requests of sincere faith, distributing the Divine Master's assistance with their best efforts. Wherever sincere and uplifting sentiments vibrate, a pathway to God's watch-care is opened."[83]

There is no discrimination amongst the many religions of the earth, all who profess a belief in God and try to light a path of love and goodness shall receive care from the spiritual realm.

Next Andre wishes to know what would happen to her if she had no religious beliefs or any other spiritual activity. Anacleto replies:

"If she were a person with upright sentiments, although hostile toward religion, in her natural meditations she would receive help, albeit reduced due to her inability to more intensely receive our radiating energies. But if she were completely immersed in the darkness of ignorance or evil, she would be without help of a higher order and her physical energies would suffer violent and inevitable wear and tear due to continuous mental intoxication. Those who close themselves off to regenerative ideas and flee from the laws of cooperation will suffer the appropriate consequences."[84]

Hence, anyone with any connection to their spiritual side will be noticed and aided by the spirit world. Only those who are completely trapped by their overwhelming materialistic thinking and behavior, or a glaring absence of love for their fellow beings are left to fend on their own. The rest of us are being supported on a frequent basis. When you wake up astonishingly refreshed after a hard day or find that one more bit of energy to survive your current trial that could be the spirit world, pushing you on with an invisible hand. A hand of warmth and love, a hand forged in the same trials which we have all been through.

## How are Spirits and People Trained to Give Passes?

Incarnate and discarnates must be trained to be able to effectively aid others through the transfer of Vital Fluids. Andre inquires about any special training or qualifications that are prerequisites to providing passes. He receives an answer:

"As they do their work, goodwill alone is not enough, as is also the case in other areas of our work. They need to display certain qualities of a superior order and certain specialized knowledge. Even when discarnate, servants of the good cannot act satisfactorily in this type of service if they cannot yet maintain a higher standard of continuous mental elevation, an indispensable condition for the exteriorization of radiant faculties. Missionaries involved in magnetic assistance, either on the physical plane or here in our sphere, must have great self-control, naturally balanced sentiments, a purified love for their fellow beings, a higher understanding of life, strong faith and a deep trust in the Divine Power."[85]

Therefore, the spirit workers undergo rigorous training to fulfill their mission. While incarnates must possess an understanding of the Doctrine of Spiritism and the required goodwill toward their fellow beings. To receive passes, requires only faith and openness to allow the refreshing waves to be absorbed into your body.

The Spiritist who is acting as the channel must also be prepared, in mind and body, as pointed out:

"Before anything else, they must balance their emotions. It isn't possible to offer constructive energies to somebody else, even if acting as a useful instrument, if one systematically wastes one's own vital radiations. A worn out and oppressed nervous system is a channel that does not respond to the interruptions that take place. Excessive bitterness, unbridled passion and obsessive anxiety are barriers that impede the passage of auxiliary energies. On the other hand, it is also necessary to examine physiological requirements as well as requisites of a psychic order. The monitoring of elements destined for the cellular reservoirs is indispensable for anyone interested in attending to the tasks of the good. Excessive eating produces fetid odors that emanate through the pores as well as through the outlets from the lungs and the stomach, harming the radiating faculties because it causes abnormal ejections and great disharmony in the gastrointestinal system, which in turn affects the inside of the cells. Alcohol and other toxic substances create disturbances in the nervous centers, altering certain psychic functions and annulling the best efforts for the transmissions of regenerative and salutary elements."[86]

As one can see, our bodies are finely tuned instruments, which are capable of actions beyond our imagination. We don't exist only to feed ourselves and procreate, but we are first and foremost devices for good, for not only by our thoughts and actions, but by maintaining the emotional and physical health of our outer covering while we are doing our time on earth. For this vehicle in which our spirit presently resides can do more than move us around in space, but is also capable of transmissions of life altering rays, benefiting our fellow humans.

The old saying, our body is a temple, is accurate. We have been bequeathed this divine apparatus to use wisely, not to abuse in a thoughtless manner. When we are assigned our trial on earth, our body is also allocated to us, much like textbooks at the start of a class. As in the school room, we are expected to keep our materials in good shape and to use them sensibly.

## The Tenth-Time Rule

Which brings us to the limit of patience extended to us by the spirit domain. As happens to us when we ignore repeated warnings, our friends give up and remain silent. Knowing in their hearts that it is a pity we are on the wrong path, but they realize that some people only learn by suffering the results of their actions. The spirit world does the same.

Andre is told when treatment is withheld:

"Our efforts are also educational and we cannot disregard the suffering that instructs and helps transform people for the good. Amongst the service rules we must follow in this center, it is crucial to determine the causes as we extirpate people's ills. There are individuals who actually induce suffering, disturbance and imbalance, and it is only reasonable that they pay for the consequences of their actions. When we come across people in such conditions, we save them from the enveloping harmful fluids, produced by their own decisions, for up to ten consecutive times as a gesture of spiritual benevolence. However, if the ten opportunities fly past without any benefit to the interested parties, we have instructions from above to let them be so that they may learn by themselves. We can give them some relief, but never free them."[87]

Andre is then given an example of a tenth-timer:

"Despite his sympathy toward our spiritual activities, this man has a difficult temperament in that he is extremely capricious. He likes to quarrel frequently, to engage in passionate arguments and to impose his points of view. He can't control his rage and constantly awakens anger and resentment in those who share his company."[88]

Hence the man is going to Spiritist lectures, reading the books and yet has not modified his behavior. He will be allowed time to come around, if he begins to take the messages of love, caring, and honesty to heart, he will once again be treated with healing passes.

We are supplied more help than we can imagine in our lives, but if we ignore the yellow flags that we have speedily passed by, then we shall be allowed the opportunity to learn the hard way. Hopefully, when we do crash down into that ditch, we will acknowledge our faults and work to better ourselves. On the other hand, if we blindly travel on, oblivious of the multitude of ominous signs, we shall have the occasion to look back at our life and try to progress in our next reincarnation.

# Chapter 14 - NDE – Near Death Experience – Michael J

Michael J had one of the most complete NDE's that I have seen. He was able to retain many memories from his experience. His revelations of the spirit world are fascinating. I take the reader through Michael's experiences and relate what the Spirit world is actually doing.

Michael J, as a result of a terrible accident when he was a young man, had an extensive NDE experience. He talked to the spirits, looked at alternative futures and was told of upcoming events. You can read his whole story at the NDERF.org website.

Michael was climbing on some limestone cliffs on a frozen day, when part of the boulder he was hanging onto suddenly broke free. He and the large rock both fell, with the boulder landing on top of him. According to Michael's recollection, the stone weighed 400-500 pounds. He felt that he left his body and seeing himself, he knew he was dead. Next Michael encounters a spirit guide:

"He told me this was an accident and I <could> go back, IF I wanted. I told him by my thoughts there was no way to make that body work. It was squashed flat. He basically told me that he could make it work again. Did I want to go back? I wanted to know my options. What would happen if I chose to go back and what would happen if I didn't. No sooner did I think these thoughts and BOOM, I was hit with a package of images. It showed in brief what would happen if I didn't go back. I saw my sister get into alcohol and drugs and her life spin out of control ... BECAUSE I wasn't there. I saw my Dad commit suicide because of my death shortly after my mom divorced him over the matter of my death. I saw my paternal grandfather wither away and die, his heart broken over my death and my dad's suicide. There were twin blows that destroyed all the joy he had left in life. The effects went on and on, my mom was sad and heart broken the rest of her life and so very lonely ...

And I saw a parade of faces of people I would never meet and whose lives I would have impacted and whose lives would have impacted mine but now I would never know any of them and they would never know me. The man in the white robe had me with my sister. I've always loved my little sister and for her alone I would have chosen to come back but seeing all that pain it would cause everyone else ... mom, dad, grandparents, friends, cousins, aunts, uncles ... man I HAD to go back." [89]

Michael's spirit guide, or guardian angel as many people call it, was right there in an instant. People who have had NDE's recognize that we live close to the spirit world. They are all around us, watching, guiding and trying to lead us to become better souls. But for most of us, the thought that spirits, or worse ghosts, inhabit the same space is a primitive notion and should be discarded, otherwise we would demonstrate to the world our ignorance and naivety. What if, these uncivilized people, who lived closer to nature and by no choice of their own, possessed little material goods, detected a truth about our sphere and the spirit realm that we have lost? Could we, who must be presented with absolute proof of everything, be missing something important, right before our eyes?

An alternative future was shown to Michael. How could this be? Allan Kardec, in his *The Spirits Book*, describes the power of a high spirit. He likens it to us, here on earth, walking through a trail in a canyon, not knowing what the next bend will look like. Whereas, the spirit, sitting on the mountain top, sees our path, where it will lead and other paths that may be offered to us. Still, this is easy to say, but how could this be in practice? What type of instantaneous mathematical calculations of probability, combined with moving pictures of those possibilities must be processed to present in life like simulation a series of future options? I have no clue, but imagining how this could be done, may be a worthwhile pursuit.

Next, Michael was shown what would happen if he chose to return to his physical body:

"Then came a second package of images, those of what would happen IF I went back. I skipped over the obvious. Dad DIDN'T commit suicide. My sister turned out Ok. Mom ended up happy. My grandfather went on to beam with pride over his first grandson to attend a university. My grandfather was a legal immigrant from Italy who never made it past the 4th grade and he treasured education beyond EVERYTHING. He crowed like a proud rooster when his kids graduated from high school and I became the first of his grandkids to attend a prestigious university. But what I focused on in this second package was what I would pay as a price for going back. I knew that I would walk again, that all I had lost would be restored but only temporarily. In my latter life, perhaps 10 to 15 years after the accident, I would suffer pain, extreme pain and it would affect me the rest of my life.

I chose to come back. He smiled, as if he KNEW I would pick the harder path because of how I felt for my family and friends. There was a snap and a pop and I was back in my body. It was FILLED with crackling electricity like sounds and feelings. I had no breath, no air and this huge rock was choking off all air. I grabbed the small end of the tear near my nose with my one free left hand (my right arm was pinned under the rock) and rolled the thing off me like it was made of paper mache`."[90]

Michael's perispirit, the connection we have from our spirit to our physical bodies, was re-attached to his broken body. From the second option presented, one can see how positive influences have far-reaching and significant effects on other people's lives. We should never underestimate our power to help. While things may appear to us to be small and unimportant, one never knows how our actions could be translated into helping or harming another person's life and those relations of that person.

Michael was next transported to the hospital, where he experienced his second phase of the NDE:

"The next thing I know I'm back in the operating room where the surgeon is working frantically to save my life and as he works at massaging my heart I found myself drifting away and the further I drifted the darker the room got and the further away his voice sounded, Found myself well above the operating theater where I should have been on a floor above that room or outside looking on a roof, but I wasn't. Instead I was floating in the entrance to a tunnel or vortex. I was sucked into it and then was when my adventure REALLY began.

I ended up with a life review, and was escorted around "the other side" by a being who was my guardian angel/teacher whom I came to call "professor" but he had an incredible sense of humor. I say "he" with tongue in cheek because "he" was neither a he or a she.

I saw what happened to true atheists (apparently I was opened minded enough that I didn't qualify). I got to see various "heavens" and asked to see what "Hell" was like if there was one (and there was but it was nothing like I expected). I even asked to meet Jesus and apologize only to meet a man that was nothing like I expected and was given interesting historical facts I was later able to verify.

But all of that is FAR TOO complex to include here, including numerous predictions of the future that have ALL come true except ONE, which I think is yet to happen"[91]

Michael's guardian angel gave him the complete tour. Michael was gifted with a life review, so in the future; he would know what type of actions stand out, in either good or bad light. People with NDE's are extremely lucky to have the opportunity to have their tests graded before the end of their allotted time, so they can improve in the second half of their test.

According to various books, psychographed by Francisco C. Xavier, and inspired by the spirit Andre Luiz, when true atheists die, meaning those who absolutely expect to never wake up again, they don't wake up. They exist in a sleep-like state, since our thoughts are our actions in the spirit world. Only with time and assistance from helpful spirits, are these souls stirred to life, and made ready for their time in the spirit world.

Michael's description of various heavens is correct. There are different levels of heavens. There are celestial cities around our planet awaiting good souls to ascend. Additionally, as we become purer spirits, there are places reserved for various levels of spirits. In fact, the whole universe is filled with colonies of spirits, each one, according to the Law of Affinity (whereby spirits who have attained similar inclinations).

As to Hell, Michael may have been to one of the locations where spirits who have committed crimes are gathered together, again caused by the Law of Affinity. I have heard one of these places described as a brutal Asian city which existed 150 years ago, somewhat dirty, slaves pulling carts, and the feeling of violence in the air. An alternative site that may have been shown to Michael could have been the Lower Zone, where spirits, who are tied to earth, still wander. The Lower Zone starts right on the surface of our planet and ascends some miles upwards, until it hits the border of the celestial cities. Now you may say, this is impossible, I look up and see nothing but sky. We cannot detect these places because they exist in a different place or dimension than us. Remember, spirits are less dense and composed of energy, while we are composed of matter.

As mentioned earlier, higher level spirits have knowledge of the future and Michael was told of certain events that would happen, and they did. All foretold events, except one, which may occur in the future, have transpired. Others may read this and think, just coincides, Michael's brain was shutting down and somehow he thought images in his mind told him all that he wrote. But ask yourself, how could he have known the future? Yes, he could have, in his imagination, visited heaven, have conversations with spirits, experienced many other sensations, but he was given concrete happenings.

Another interesting comment was made by Michael in his report. At the end of the description of a NDE, there is a series of questions posed to the person who is reporting the event.

**"At what time during the experience were you at your**

**highest level of consciousness and alertness?** After I was clear of my body, BOTH times. As I said before, I have an IQ of about 150, genius level and yet when out of my body, in a "dead" state, I found myself WAY smarter. Comparing the two. I'd consider myself a drooling moron to what I was outside my limiting body."[92]

When you are pure energy, think of the power of your mind. Think of what you know now and realize that you know nothing. Think of the reality people say you should acknowledge and inside you consider that they have no clue about the real reality. We are but a physical speck of dust, on earth to learn the correct attitudes so the vast resources of our intellectual ability can be put to good use.

Lastly, Michael gives an answer to one of the questions, which I believe illustrates how we all connect and how God hears our prayers and sees all:

"**During your experience, did you encounter any specific information / awareness that a mystical universal connection or unity/oneness either does (or does not) exist?** Yes I EXPERIENCED that universal connection. We are both part of a great supernatural "internet" and yet simultaneously separate PCs as well (to use an analogy)."[93]

In the book, *In the Realms of Mediumship*, psychographed by Francisco C. Xavier and inspired by the spirit Emmanuel, the Preface of the book written by Emmanuel, tells us;

"Through the sentiments that characterize their inner life, all individuals emit specific rays and live within the spiritual wave with which they identify themselves.

Such truths cannot remain semi-hidden in our sanctuaries of faith; they will radiate from the temples of science like mathematical equations."[94]

Hence, Michael is describing the concept of the Internet, where we all have a unique identifier and we are in constant

94

communication with all around us. Our minds are constantly transmitting information which the spirit world receives. Our waking conscious may not be able to decipher the code, although some people have fleeting moments of intuition that make it through our physical filters.

In summary, Michael's NDE substantiates, independently of the Doctrine of Spiritism, the complex and overwhelming power of the hidden world around us. The Druids called it the "Other World", for they too knew that we are but temporary casings housing an immortal soul.

# Section 3 – How does all of this Work

Now that you have learned that our lives are mapped out and we have assistance from the Spirit world in our classroom on earth, you need to know how all of this exists. What is the organization of the spirit world, who communicated this to us, and how does it all work?

Unlike the ancient religions where the information was sequestered in the priestly class and only exposed to others for a specific purpose, Spiritism, as well as Christianity and Judaism before it, attempted to present all revelations and knowledge to whoever cared to read it.

The availability of the disclosures of the spirit world has always been their objective. The spirit world has had to struggle against human nature to use any lever for power and personal gain. Time and time again moral and civic codes that should have been guidelines for all have been suppressed.

This is why one of the aims of the spirit world is the rise of Western Civilization, which, although brought about the ravages of colonization, enabled vast technological advances and most importantly, the rise of the educated classes. The result, which typifies this phenomenon, is the Protestant Revolution. Once the Bible was made widely available, people were able to supply their own interpretations. Hence, their dependency on paying indulgences to church officials became obsolete, when they knew such payments altered nothing.

Of course people being what they are, all of this led to years of wars labeled by historians as the Protestant Reformation and then the Counter Reformation by the Catholic Church. Since the Counter Reformation did not achieve all of its objectives, it then morphed into the Inquisition, whose purpose was to torture or eliminate any possible heretic before they multiplied beyond a manageable number.

All unfolding under the watchful eyes of our spirit guides, who would be forgiven if they had just given up there and then. Lucky for us, our trajectory of progress, brutality and some more progress was known in advance and planned for in detail. For they well understood that the human race doesn't receive a message and acts on it. First we ignore, and then when the possibility of real change is on the horizon, we try to violently stamp it out. Next, when the idea becomes a fait accompli, people in power try to both adapt it to fit or corrupt the messengers and absorb them into the ruling elite.

Hence, as you shall see, we have had multiple prophets and wise men, all with a common core of beliefs. It is no accident that Confucius, Socrates and Jesus have all said in effect; Do unto others what you want others to do unto you. Socrates' version was more along the lines of "It has been shown that to injure anyone is never just anywhere"[95]. While Confucius stated, "Never impose on others what you would not choose for yourself". All analogous and all convey the central meaning of the importance of practicing fair behavior toward your fellow human. This sentiment is mirrored in Buddhism, Baha'i, Hinduism and Islam.

Others look at the similarities and accuse religious figures of plagiarizing, while the truth is that all are guided by the spirit world to stay on message. With the hope of someday, we may actually listen and take on such behavior in our everyday life.

Hence, we shall survey what is Spiritism, what are its major tenets and who were the leading figures bringing this vital wisdom to us. For not only was the Doctrine of Spiritism telegraphed to us back in the days of Socrates, four hundred years before Christ, and later codified in the 1850's by Allan Kardec, but even today we are continuously being fed more information. Revealing ever more fascinating aspects of our spirit life; our real life when we aren't in our physical bodies.

The spirit world does more than send us valuable knowledge and guides us individually toward our destiny. Their involvement in the entire human existence on earth is pervasive. Not only do they work with and on us, putting us on the assembly line to perfection; filtering out our impurities, but they also send us souls to be reincarnated with specific missions. Missions which are meant to raise our political, spiritual, and technological levels. How we are managed on a grand scale is discussed in this section. There is a campaign for improving the entire planet. A massive effort that would make our collection of the world's armies seems trivial. There was a start to the operation and there is an end goal. Participants are mobilized and trained across the span of centuries, always with the aim of pushing us forward to a just society.

# Chapter 15 – What is the Doctrine of Spiritism

This chapter is an introduction to Spiritism. What you should know about the beginnings and the doctrine of Spiritism before you decide to become a Spiritist.

In essence, your soul will live forever. You will experience life after life in a quest to perfect yourself. You have a mission, the most important mission possible; to improve, to love, to be charitable. To be part of a grand plan to not only raise yourself, but your neighbors and the entire human race.

While in the spirit world we are bathed in love, each of us must learn how to love. Hence, for every wrong you commit, you will have to pay for it in this life or the next. And, the trials you are experiencing now are the results of errors you have committed in the past, plus a splattering of coursework that you have been assigned. Our suffering is for the noble cause of teaching us to love unconditionally.

How do we know all of this?

## Jesus promised us more Information

"If you love me, keep my commands.  And I will ask the Father, and he will give you another Consoler to help you and be with you forever…the Spirit of Truth. The world cannot accept him, because it neither sees him nor knows him. But you know him, for he lives with you and will be in you." New Testament John 14: 15-17

"But the Consoler, the Holy Spirit, whom the Father will send in my name, will teach you all things and will remind you of everything I have said to you." New Testament John 14: 26

What did the Consoler actually do? What did he contribute? Spiritism states that Allan Kardec was the Codifier, who presented the Spirit of Truth (Consoler) and that in the five books that Allan Kardec assembled, he revealed the extent of the Spirit world, who is God and Jesus, why we are here on earth, how we should live and the doctrine to follow. That is all. The answers to questions that every one of us have spent nights pondering.

## What is Spiritism?

The basic tenants of Spiritism are:

1. Love God.

2. Do unto others as you would have others do unto you.

3. Practice justice.

4. Forgive all who offend you.

5. Make amends for our own wrong doing.

The spirits revealed to us the basic facts of our existence:

1. Your soul is immortal.

2. You travel through multiple lives as a process to learn to love, be fraternal, and be selfless.

3. The goal of God is for every spirit to one day be pure.

4. There is no eternal hell, it is a station for souls who are materialistic and have an excessive love of self.

5. There are many levels of heaven. Heaven is not a place where we have eternal leisure, but one of on-going work to help others.

6. Life on earth is like a school. You are assigned events in your life and how you react and behave will determine your spiritual progress.

In the 1930's in Brazil, the medium Chico Xavier began psychographing (the process of a medium writing under the direction of a spirit) messages and books sent by spirits. From the very beginning he was told to always follow the doctrines of Allan Kardec. Chico wrote more than 400 books by the time of his death in 2002. Within these books, the Spirits revealed information about Allan Kardec and the Spirit world's plan for our future:

1. When Jesus referred to the "Great Consoler", he was foretelling the arrival of the Spirit of Truth, which was codified by Allan Kardec.

2. For the earth to progress, the human race needs to understand that every action they do here on earth will have consequences in their next life.

3. The Bible was written by men under the influence of their beliefs and culture at their time. While the central spiritual message of love is eternal, the stories of the Bible, such as the Earth being made in six days are allegories and not meant to be taken literally.

4. We are being told this now because the human race is culturally and technically advanced to be able to accept these messages.

5. Spiritism is not meant to replace religions, but to supplement them with the knowledge of the basic doctrine of reincarnation and its purpose.

6. The spreading and acceptance of Spiritism will enable the world to begin a new age, where war is a thing of the past.

7. The Spirit world has planned these events and is guiding the earth through subtle interventions.

8. At some time in the future, science will definitely prove the existence of a soul and an afterlife.

As one can see, the tenets of reincarnation have also been delivered to us via an alternative channel. That of the spirit world communicating directly to mediums to alert us of a life beyond our single human existence. While all around us people who have psychic abilities or those who had NDEs experiences are reporting the same philosophy of love and redemption through trials.

# Chapter 16 - Allan Kardec – The Codifier of Spiritism

Allan Kardec is the pen name of the French teacher and educator Hippolyte Léon Denizard Rivail (Lyon, October 3, 1804 – Paris, March 31, 1869).[96] Wikipedia describes his early life:

Rivail was born in Lyon in 1804. He was raised as a Catholic. He was a disciple and collaborator of Johann Heinrich Pestalozzi, and a teacher of mathematics, physics, chemistry, astronomy, physiology, comparative anatomy and French in Paris. For one of his research papers, he was inducted in 1831 into the Royal Academy of Arras. He organized and taught free courses for the underprivileged.

On February 1832, he married Amélie Gabrielle Boudet. Rivail became a convert to Spiritism in May, 1855 after attending a séance where he claimed to witness table-turning which he believed was caused by spirits.[97]

Anna Blackwell, in her forward of her translation, describes the numerous achievements he made, before he became exposed to Spiritism:

Of the numerous educational works published by him may be mentioned, A Plan for the Improvement of Public Instruction, submitted by him in 1828 to the French Legislative Chamber, by which body it was highly extolled, though not acted upon; A Course of Practical and Theoretic Arithmetic, on the Pestalozzian System, for the use of Teachers and Mothers (1829); A Classical Grammar of the French Tongue (1831); A Manual for the use of Candidates for Examination in the Public Schools; with Explanatory Solutions of various Problems of Arithmetic and Geometry (1848); Normal Dictations for the Examinations of the Hotel de Ville and the Sorbonne, with Special Dictations on Orthographic Difficulties (1849) These works, highly esteemed at the time of their publication, are still in use in many French schools; and their author was bringing out new editions of some of them at the time of his death.[98]

Allan Kardec, for I will use his pen name from now on, was fifty-one years old when he first encountered spirits. Anna Blackwell, who translated his books into English in 1881, describes his first encounters and what set him off in his journey:

"When, about 1850, the phenomenon of "table-turning" was exciting the attention of Europe and ushering in the other phenomena since known as "spiritist", he quickly divined the real nature of those phenomena, as evidence of the existence of an order of relationships hitherto suspected rather than known, namely, those which unite the visible and invisible worlds. Foreseeing the vast importance, to science and to religion, of such an extension of the field of human observation, he entered at once upon a careful investigation of the new phenomena. A friend of his had two daughters who had become what are now called "mediums." They were gay, lively, amiable girls, fond of society, dancing, and amusement, and habitually received, when "sitting" by themselves or with their young companions, "communications" in harmony with their worldly and somewhat frivolous disposition. But, to the surprise of all concerned, it was found that, whenever he was present, the messages transmitted through these young ladies were of a very grave and serious character; and on his inquiring of the invisible intelligences as to the cause of this change, he was told that "spirits of a much higher order than those who habitually communicated through the two young mediums came expressly for him, and would continue to do so, in order to enable him to fulfill an important religious mission."[99]

He was extremely interested in this message of a mission and wished to delve deeper. He discussed how he could ask and organize a series of questions to get a more complete understanding of the spirit world with his wife. His wife, Amelie, encouraged him to undertake this task. Given his background, he organized a series of questions that would be posed by mediums to spirits. Allan Kardec was not a medium himself, so he used the service of various mediums to gather the information. He did not rely on one reply, but made sure that an answer to one question was seconded by another medium in a different location. Anna Blackwell recounts the sequence of events that led him to publish:

When these conversations had been going on for nearly two years, he one day remarked to his wife, in reference to the unfolding of these views, which she had followed with intelligent sympathy: "It is a most curious thing! My conversations with the invisible intelligences have completely revolutionized my ideas and convictions. The instructions thus transmitted constitute an entirely new theory of human life, duty, and destiny, that appears to me to be perfectly rational and coherent, admirably lucid and consoling, and intensely interesting. I have a great mind to publish these conversations in a book; for it seems to me that what interests me so deeply might very likely prove interesting to others." His wife warmly approving the idea, he next submitted it to his unseen interlocutors, who replied in the usual way, that it was they who had suggested it to his mind, that their communications had been made to him, not for himself alone, but for the express purpose of being given to the world as he proposed to do, and that the time had now come for putting this plan into execution. "To the book in which you will embody our instructions," continued the communicating intelligences, "you will give, as being our work rather than yours, the title of Le Livre des Esprits (The Spirits' Book); and you will publish it, not under your own name, but under the pseudonym of Allan Kardec. Keep your own name of Rivail for your own books already published; but take and keep the name we have now given you for the book you are about to publish by our order, and, in general, for all the work that you will have to do in the fulfillment of the mission which, as we have already told you, has been confided to you by Providence, and which will gradually open before you as you proceed in it under our guidance."[100]

From this scholarly pursuit, all five books were created. In the fourteen years of his life that he codified the doctrine of Spiritism, he traveled spreading the word and helped organize many

Spiritism societies and created a Spiritism magazine. He endured much skepticism and abuse from many in society and from the Catholic and Protestant churches. Organized religion would spend the next hundred years trying to stamp out Spiritism with all of their might. Almost succeeding, except for the outpost of Brazil, which has brought the doctrine back to life and is currently on a mission to expand its reach.

Allan Kardec's death was sudden and peaceful, on the night that he had just finished drawing up the constitution and rules for his Spiritist Society, seated at his desk in his apartment in Paris, he died of an aneurysm. His wife dedicated herself to the continuation of his work.

## Allan Kardec's Books

Allan Kardec wrote five books (The Spirits' Book, 1857; The Mediums' Book, 1861; The Gospel according to Spiritism, 1864; Heaven and Hell, 1865; Genesis, 1868), each dealing with separate subjects, but at the same time overlapping in their complete description of the Spiritist doctrine. The first and most famous is the book that he was given the title by his spirit messengers. I took the description of each book straight from the synopsis published on Amazon.

**The Spirits Book** - Written by Allan Kardec, in 1857, is widely regarded as the most important piece of writing in the Spiritist canon. *The Spirits Book* lays out the doctrine of the belief system. The subjects that Kardec discusses lays down the foundations for the Spiritist philosophy and all of the concepts that would become, and still are, key to the movement's thinking have their genesis in the book. The belief that there is one Supreme Being, God, who created everything in the universe, is postulated. According to the text the Devil does not exist and Jesus is a messenger of God. Although the book does not refer to Jesus as the son of God and no mention is made of the 'immaculate conception' he is considered God's perfect messenger and his teachings are to be adhered to. Reincarnation and the survival of the soul after death are vital beliefs and it is stated that it is through reincarnation that lessons are learnt that can be taken into the next life and that every life moves the soul closer to perfection. According to the book man is made up of three separate elements; the body, the spirit and the spiritual body.[101]

**The Mediums Book** - The Mediums' Book is the second of the five books comprising the Codification of the Spiritist Doctrine. The book presents the teachings of the Spirits on all types of spirit manifestations, the ways of communicating with the invisible world, the different types of mediums, the development of mediumship, and the difficulties and obstacles that may be found in the practice of Spiritism. At the end of the book there is a helpful basic Spiritist glossary. Besides being a source of indispensable reading and research for Spiritists, The Mediums' Book is also an essential source of knowledge for any person interested in the mediumistic phenomenon, which is manifesting increasingly the world over, both inside and outside Spiritist activities per se. Since incarnates are an integral part of the exchange between the two planes of life- the physical and the spiritual- it is advisable that we fully understand the mechanics of such a relationship. The Mediums' Book is the safest guide for all those who have devoted themselves to communicating with the Spirit World.[102]

**The Gospel According to Spiritism** - The Gospel according to Spiritism is the third of the five books that comprise the Spiritist Codification, a compilation of teachings transmitted by high order spirits (the Spirits) and organized and commented on by Allan Kardec. The book contains the essence of the moral teachings of Jesus, thus providing a roof under which followers of all religions- even those who profess no religion at all- can gather, for it offers a sure guide for our inner reform, which, according to Christ, is indispensable for us to find future happiness and inner peace, a state that is possible for the spirit on its evolutionary journey to God only by complying fully with the divine laws.[103]

**Heaven and Hell** – The fourth book of five books, published in 1865. In this book, Allan Kardec approaches divine justice from the point of view of Spiritism. The first part is a comparative analysis of the concepts of different faiths about heaven, purgatory and hell, angels and demons, and future punishment and rewards. The dogma of eternal punishment is especially discussed and refuted by arguments taken from the laws of nature. The second part presents numerous communications with spirits in different situations, and which shed light on the state of the soul after death and its passage from the physical life to the spirit life, which until then had been obscure and feared. It is a sort of travel guide to be used before we enter a new world.[104]

**Genesis** - Genesis is the last of the five basic books of the Spiritist Codification. When studied and understood, it offers a unique opportunity for delving into great themes of universal interest, discussed in a logical, rational and revealing manner. The book is divided into three parts: the first analyzes the origin of planet earth and avoids mysterious or magical interpretations about its creation; the second deals with the question of miracles by explaining the true nature of the fluids and the extraordinary phenomena portrayed in the Gospels; the third part focuses on the predictions in the Gospels, the signs of the times and the new generation, whose advent will be the beginning of a new era for humankind, based on the practice of justice, peace and fraternity. The subjects presented in its eighteen chapters are based on the immutability of the great Divine Laws.[105]

## How Allan Kardec Wrote His Books

Allan Kardec was the codifier and the Spirit of Truth supplied the initiative for the third revelation, but do you wish to know how exactly Allan Kardec worked with the spirit world and published his books?

Allan Kardec brought us the third revelation, for this the world will always owe him our eternal gratitude. For those who have read the Bible and attempted to completely understand the meanings of the parables and phrases that could make sense from many different angles, the books published by Allan Kardec clears the fog completely. For the first time we actually are allowed to understand the processes and sociology of the spirit world. How is it maintained, who governs it, how do we get there and how do we become successful citizens of that marvelous place. It is as if the human race went from elementary school, where we learn by various methods to coach children to want to comprehend, such as play-acting, watching others, activities are planned to satisfy our short attention spans; to college, where the professor lays out what is required for the course and expects you to read the material, study it, and have the ability to pass the test at the end.

How did Allan Kardec derive and categorize this information? He utilized his science and mathematical background to gather data points from as many different locations as possible. Allan Kardec knew that for the human race to believe what is in the Doctrine, it must be the product of many. For as he says:

"If the Spirits who have revealed it had manifested to only one person, nothing would guarantee it origin, for it would be necessary to believe the word of whoever stated that he or she had received their teachings. Admitting perfect sincerity on his or her part would at most convince a circle of acquaintances; he or she would have followers but would never succeed in rallying everyone."[106]

Next he takes this concept further, and stipulates the Doctrine must be the work of many spirits. For given the answers to questions he had posed before, he understood that like humans, spirits are of different capabilities and levels. Hence, to tap into the collective knowledge of the spirit world a variety of spirits, with their own spheres of expertise, must be utilized to insure to correctness of the doctrine. Allan Kardec lays out his logic:

"It is known that, as a consequence of the differences that exist in their capabilities, spirits are far from being in possession of the whole truth individually that it is not given to all to grasp certain mysteries; that knowledge is proportional to their purification; that ordinary spirits do not know any more than humans and even less than some amongst them, as amongst the latter, there are presumptuous and pseudo-learned spirits who think they know what they in fact do not, and theorizers who take their own ideas for the truth; in short, that spirits of the highest order – those who are completely dematerialized – are the only ones divested of earthly ideas and prejudices."[107]

Lastly, using various numbers of mediums and spirits he applies the concordance rule. Different spirits working with independent mediums must illustrate similar answers to the same questions. Allan Kardec spells it out:

"The only true guarantee for spirits' teachings is in the overall agreement amongst revelations made spontaneously through a large number of mediums unknown to one other and in several places."[108]

The above is the basis for all of Allan Kardec's books. Multiple sources of revelations and similarity between the messages is the cornerstone of Spiritism. Where other theories may rely on one source, the theory may be refuted by later messages or by different spirits. Spiritism stands on a solid foundation of bedrock, not the work or ideas of one person, but the cumulative work of many on both sides, those living and those in the spirit world. Allan Kardec describes the ultimate test of the Doctrine, the ability to withstand contradiction:

"The universal test is a guarantee for the future unity of Spiritism and will annul all contradictory theories. It is in this universal test that in the future the criterion for truth will be sought."[109]

For up to the present day, one hundred and sixty years or so, the world has seen mainly confirmation of the Doctrine. What arguments that have been against Spiritism is mainly against the entire concept of learning from spirits, not the central messages of the need for love and charity. This is not to say that we will not learn more at some future time. For Allan Kardec explains that while we here on earth have evolved enough to understand the Doctrine, there is still more:

"Highly evolved spirits proceed with extreme wisdom in their revelations; they do not address the great issues of the Doctrine except gradually, to the degree that our intelligence is capable of comprehending truths of a higher order and when circumstances are propitious for the release of new ideas. That is why at the beginning they did not say everything and why they still have not said everything today, nor have they given in to the impatience of hasty individuals who would like to harvest the fruit before it is ripe."[110]

We have seen his words come true, for around one-hundred years after his publications; we now have additional works from Francisco (Chico) Xavier which expose so much detail of the daily life of the spirits who toil in their work to bring us enlightenment. In more than four-hundred books, the mysteries of the spirit world are again being slowly revealed to us. Now it is up to us to learn, to grow, to act in accordance with the Doctrine.

# Chapter 17 - Chico Xavier – Presenting us more lessons from the Spirit World

The next great movement forward for Spiritism, after Allan Kardec, was Francisco C. Xavier, also affectionately known as "Chico". Many people do not know about Chico Xavier. He revived the pursuit of the Spiritist doctrine by the world, after organized religion did their best to squash it. Through Chico, the spirit realm has more fully revealed what life is actually like after death and precisely how the process of multiple lives functions. You may not hear his name on every street corner, but later in the 21st century you will.

There have been many books and even one movie about Chico Xavier. This modest chapter is intended to present a brief survey of his life and the miraculous achievements that has defined him. The most important fact upfront to know about Chico is that the vast majority of the money made from the sale of his books went to charity. He lived very modestly, although he had people helping him constantly, cleaning his room, preparing meals, planning out his days, all so he could focus on his mission on earth – Helping us to discover the word of God and the doctrine of Spiritism.

## Childhood

Chico was born on April 2, 1910, to João Cândido Xavier (a lottery ticket vendor) and Maria João de Deus.[111] Chico demonstrated his ability to talk to the spirits at an early age. When he was four year old, after returning from a long walk back from Church to the family's home, he heard his father gossiping about a neighbor woman who had a natural abortion of her child. Not liking the tone of his father's gossip, he told his astonished parents that the abortion was due to an ectopic pregnancy and therefore unavoidable.[112] His father remarked that they must have brought home the wrong boy from church.

At the age of five, his mother died. Unable to care alone for his nine children, Chico's father split the children up amongst various friends and family. Chico went to his godmother, who was an extremely cruel person. She spanked and tortured Chico. She would stab him with a fork in his stomach and not let him pull it out.[113] He only gained solace during these times by speaking with the spirit of his dead mother.

Thankfully, his father remarried, to a wonderful woman, Cidália Batista, who agreed to marry only if João would reunite all of his children. From then until the time of her death, when Chico was seventeen, Chico possessed his greatest support among the living. He had to work at an early age supporting his large extended family. Finally in 1924, while working, he finished primary school, afterwards he never went back.[114] In 1927, his step-mother passed away, in May of the same year, his mother directed to him to read Allan Kardec's *The Spirits Book*.

## Psychographing Books

Wikipedia describes the beginning of his early writing:

In 1931, In Pedro Leopoldo, (Francisco's hometown) he started to psychograph the book Parnaso de Além-Túmulo. That year was marked by the medium's "adulthood", it was the year the medium met his spiritual mentor Emmanuel, "Under a tree, near a water reservoir..." (SOUTO MAIOR, 1995:31). His mentor informs him on his mission to psychograph a sequence of thirty books and the spirit explains to him that, to achieve such a task, it would be demanded three very important conditions: 'discipline, discipline and discipline'.

Severe and demanding, the mentor instructed him to be loyal to Jesus and Kardec, even if it was against his religious basis. Later on, the medium found out that Emmanuel had been the Roman senator Publius Lentulus, further reborn as a slave who sympathized with Christianity, still in another reincarnation, had been a Jesuit priest Manuel da Nóbrega, involved with the evangelization of Brazil.[115]

Chico was attacked by many as being one of a large legion of

113

imposters, whose only aim was to increase his personal wealth. Chico said that he could never fall down, since he never stood up, meaning that he couldn't be charged as a money seeking person because he never took money. All proceeds from his books were donated to charity. As a Spiritist, he knew that selling his services that he received as a gift from God is immoral.

The range of books written by Chico was enormous. From books by deceased poets, suicides, a young man describing learning at a school in heaven, to books by Emmanuel, which were past lives of people he knew while he was on earth. Including, Emmanuel's first encounter with Jesus Christ, in which he at first completely rejected Jesus. An interesting series of books, were by the physician Dr. Andre Luiz, who wrote about his own death and experiences in the lower zones and his entrance into Nosso Lar (the Spirit City above Rio de Janeiro) and subsequently his experiences with assisting various departments and their work in heaven, on the earth, and one below the earth.

Chico was the first person to tell the world, that he never wrote anything, he only wrote what was communicated to him by the spirit realm. He wrote a total of 469 books before he died, on June 30, 2002. His death occurred right after Brazil won the World Cup. He had wished that he would die on day that wouldn't make the Brazilians too unhappy.

### Chico Xavier the Man

Notice, that originally, Emmanuel give Chico a goal of thirty books. In Geraldo's lecture on Chico, he tells that when Chico finished his quota of thirty books, his spirit mentor Emmanuel told Chico, "Now that you have finished thirty books, how about doubling that to get to a goal of sixty books?"

"No problem", replied Chico. Then when Chico reached that goal, Emmanuel asked, "Why not go to one hundred books?"

Again, Chico said, "No problem."

Chico reached his one hundredth book around the time when

he was sixty. He wanted to retire, however, his spirit guide, Emmanuel, told him that he had bad news for Chico, Jesus had decreed that Chico will spend the rest of his life writing more books. Chico liked to tease and responded, "Well, we have freewill, don't we?"

"Of course you have freewill, you can choose not to write more books." replied Emmanuel.

"Then, I don't wish to write more books." Chico responded.

Emmanuel then told Chico, "In that case I have a second decree from Jesus, if you don't wish to write more books, then your life will end tomorrow."

Chico laughed and said, "No, no, no, I will write more books."[116]

As stated before, Chico eventually wrote 469 books. This goes to show you that in heaven as well as on earth, the reward for good work is more work. Not only did he write, but he spent a couple of nights a week, writing out messages from the spirit world to people who came to his house in search of comforting news about their deceased son, daughter, husband, or wife. He would go from early evening to four or five in the morning during these sessions. Afterwards, he would want to talk to his support staff like it was lunch time. Geraldo was part of the people who helped him, and he was amazed at the stamina of Chico.[117]

Geraldo also listened to Chico tell about the depth of love that Jesus and all of the spirit world has for all of us. Chico loved all of us, he would go to bed at night thinking of the people he wanted to pray for, and go from house to house, praying for people in his mind until the dawn came.

Chico was able to foretell the future. Geraldo tells of a time in the mid-1980s when Chico told a group that Brazil would be a major oil exporter and that the oil would be found over 5000 meters under the sea. Everyone silently laughed, they had had plenty of experience of the Brazilian government trying to find oil and nothing ever was successful.[118] Now, of course, Brazil is a major oil producer from fields of oil found out in the deep ocean.

In summary, Chico lived a hard, but a fulfilled life. He demonstrated his love for all us over and over. He accomplished his mission while on earth, with very little reward while he was with us. He was sent by the spirit world to expose more information about how the spirit realm works, what does it mean to each of us, and for all to realize that adherence to the golden rule, "Do unto others as you would have them do unto you", love for your fellow beings, and living an honorable life are the keys to enter heaven. Where, we are not at eternal leisure, but at eternal work, work to help others advance themselves as we advance through the trials of successive lives.

# Chapter 18 - Socrates - Preparing the way for Christianity and Spiritism

Chico Xavier represents the most recent face of Spiritism. We have explored how he greatly increased the communications and knowledge from the spirit realm to the human race. There wasn't just these two supplying the information for us to digest. There were more, a precursor to not only Christianity, but to Spiritism as well, more than 400 years before Christ brought us the second revelation.

Allan Kardec in the book, *The Gospel According to Spiritism*, lays out the philosophy of Socrates as recorded by Plato. The basic doctrine of Socrates is very similar to what Jesus preached and Spiritism codified. Which should not be surprising, since all had their headwaters in the same place; the spirit world.

Socrates was born in Athens, Greece, sometime in the years 470 or 469 BC and lived 71 years until his death by state execution in the year 399 BC.[119] He was executed by the state for questioning the use of power by Athens and his supposedly bad influence on the youth of the day. His major crime was to object to the rule of "might makes right" and his exposure of follies by the leaders of Athens.[120] An example of the teachings of Socrates, as reported by Plato, which may have been objectionable to the ruling citizens of Athens is:

"One should never return injustice for injustice, nor do evil to anyone, whatever may be the evil they have done to us."[121]

More than 400 years before Christ, Socrates was telling us to learn to live with one another and to forgive others without hesitation. Socrates believed the best way for people to live was to focus on the pursuit of virtue rather than the pursuit of material wealth.[122] The message of forgiveness and self-improvement could be taken verbatim from the New Testament or the Doctrine of Spiritism.

Socrates goes on the explain what is important to God:

"The most beautiful prayers and the most beautiful sacrifices please the Divinity less than a virtuous soul who puts forth the effort to resemble it. It would be a grave thing if the gods were to have more consideration for our offerings than for our soul. This way, even the guiltiest could render themselves favorable. But no, there are no truly just and wise except those who through their work and deeds redeem what they owe to the gods and men."[123]

This is the message that has been repeated again and again to us, by philosophers from China, Persia, India, Greece, Israel, and lastly France via Allan Kardec. Are these persons plagiarizing one another throughout the centuries or is it the spirit world sending us the wisdom that we all need to acquire to better ourselves?

## Reincarnation

Socrates also knew that we are immortal souls, who go through periods incarnated on earth:

"While we have our body, and as long as our soul is immersed in this corruption, we will never possess the object of our desire: the truth. In fact the body brings forth in us a thousand obstacles due to our need to care for it. Moreover, it fills us with desire, appetites, fears, a thousand chimeras and a thousand follies, so that, while in it, it is impossible to be wise, even for an instant. However, since it is not possible to know anything purely while the soul is united with the body, one of two things will happen: either we will never know the truth, or we will only come to know it after death. Freed from the insanity of the body, we then will converse – hopefully – with individuals likewise freed, and we will know for ourselves the essence of things. That is why true philosophers prepare themselves to die, and why death is no way seems fearsome to them."[124]

Death is the great freedom. We are free from our material form, we are free from the trials we signed up for, and we are free from hate, jealousy, hunger, and pain. We are free to think and be with others we love and respect. A revelation given to us in *The Spirits Book*, but has also been in front of us for the last 2500 years in the Dialogues of Plato.

Socrates also knew what happens after death, where we are interrogated; discuss our lessons learned and lessons failed, spend our time in the spirit world, then after the allotted interval we construct the plan for our next life. Socrates describes it thusly:

"After our deaths, the spirit (*daimon*) who had been assigned to us during life leads us to a place where all those who must be taken to Hades are gathered in order to be judged. After having remained in Hades for the time required, souls are re-conducted to this life for numerous and long periods."[125]

## Parallels with Jesus

Socrates dedicated himself to pursuit of knowledge, via a series of questions, each one meant to find what was wrong with the previous answer, or contradicted other statements to get to the truth. He believed the quest for knowledge was our primary duty and only thus could we temporarily escape the torments and wants of our physical existence. By his rigorous thought processes he tried to enable people to comprehend the beauty in spiritual growth and the transitory nature of material wealth. On wealth he said; "Wealth is a great danger. All who love wealth love neither themselves nor what they are, but something that is even more foreign to them than what they are."[126]

How like the teachings of Jesus, who gave us the image of a camel passing through the eye of a needle to the chances of a rich person attaining heaven. For when we worship that which is of this earth, we are unable to lift our thoughts to higher matters, for with wealth we must deal with the daily pressures to protect our goods, contend with numerous enemies who are after our assets, and plot our next steps.

119

Socrates also understood our failings to examine ourselves, when he was recorded saying, "It is a natural disposition in each of us to perceive our own defects much less than those of others."[127] The parallels with Jesus' admonishing us that we see the speck in our neighbor's eye, but not the plank in our own eye, is telling. These are not just two random men with similar philosophies, but a concerted effort by the spiritual world to reveal how to comport ourselves in order to prepare our souls for advancement.

His dialogues, written and publish by Plato, remain treasures of logical thought and philosophy even today. We can all learn from the wisdom of the Athenian philosopher, whose Socratic dialogue process formed the basis of the scientific method and taught us to constantly assess where we are, who we are, and how are we improving and acquiring knowledge on a daily basis.

Like Jesus, Socrates in his pursuit to lead us onto the right path, suffered obstruction from enemies of enlightenment, and both in the end were condemned to die by the state. Allan Kardec lived in a more advanced society where non-believers weren't struck down, but merely ridiculed, shunned, and repressed by the state and church.

We too live in a time, when the teachings of Spiritism and words of spirituality will cause a wave of aversion to our ideals. Where the mere mention of God is seen as an insult to someone and must be punished. We aren't even given the gift of being ignored if one doesn't like our message. Through all of the verbal assaults, we must like thousands of adherents before us be strong and know in our hearts that our message of love, fraternity, charity and the active participation of God's workers in our daily lives will someday be heard.

# Chapter 19 - Emanuel Swedenborg – Advance Man for Allan Kardec

We have learned about Allan Kardec and his *The Spirits Book*, which started the Spiritist movement and laid out the doctrine of Spiritism. But, did you know the Spirit World prepared the way for Allan Kardec? Just as Socrates and John the Baptist led the way for Jesus Christ. The same process was implemented for Kardec, and his name was Emanuel Swedenborg and what he wrote at the time caused a major scandal.

I first heard the name of Swedenborg, when I was reading the book *Workers of the Life Eternal*, psychographed by Francisco C. Xavier and inspired by the spirit Andre Luiz. One of the more evolved spirits was giving a lecture concerning the communication between the spirit world and the people of earth, when he said:

> "Swedenborg, the great medium, traverses a few sections of our zones of action and portrays the customs of the 'astral dwelling' as best he can, engraving on the narratives the strong characteristics of his personal concepts."[128]

My first reaction was, is this person real? Whenever I chance across a historical name in any of the spiritual books that I am not familiar with, I attempt to verify their existence. Sometimes, I am successful and other times, the names are too obscure and lost in the fog of history. Therefore, I immediately looked him up on the internet and was very surprised with what I found. Before he became a medium and interested in the spirit world, he was a successful scientist. He did not begin investigating the spiritual world until he was 57. The story of his dramatic moment of revelation is intriguing; but keep in mind Swedenborg himself did not verify in writing these events, only verbally to his friends.

> "In April 1745, Swedenborg was dining in a private room at a tavern in London. By the end of the meal, a darkness fell upon his eyes, and the room shifted character. Suddenly he saw a person sitting at a corner of the room, telling Swedenborg: "*Do*

*not eat too much!*". Swedenborg, scared, hurried home. Later that night, the same man appeared in his dreams. The man told Swedenborg that He was the Lord, that He had appointed Swedenborg to reveal the spiritual meaning of the Bible, and that He would guide Swedenborg in what to write. The same night, the spiritual world was opened to Swedenborg."[129]

Reading this, I wanted to discover more about him and his ideas.

## Life before his revelation

Emanuel Swedenborg was born in Stockholm, Sweden, on January 29, 1688. He was the second son of a pastor, in Sweden's Lutheran state church. His father was also a university professor, where at the age of eleven Emanuel entered the university where his father taught. He graduated in 1709, at the age of 21. He came from a wealthy family; therefore he could travel after college. He went to London where he traveled in the same circles as Sir Isaac Newton and Edmund Halley.[130]

Swedenborg made a name for himself by publishing several scientific books on Metallurgy, plus a book on iron and one about copper and brass. He also wrote a book on Anatomy. The first volume addresses the heart and blood; the second, the brain, nervous system, and the soul.[131] Throughout this time he worked on Sweden's Board of Mines, which enabled him time to pursue his scientific work.

Hence, similar to Allan Kardec, Emanuel Swedenborg was no mere peasant with vision, but a published scholar, a man of means, who lived in a circle of some of the greatest minds of the 18th century.

## Life after his revelation

Two years after his revelation, in 1747, he asked to be released from his duties so he could work full time revealing the spirit world to humanity. The first volume he wrote, *Secrets of Heaven*, was published in London in 1749; the eighth and final volume was published in 1756.[132]

His initial sales of the books were disappointing, but starting in 1759, a series of events occurred, which piqued the interest of society and pushed his name and books to the forefront. At a dinner party in Goteborg, Sweden, he suddenly became agitated and began describing a fire in Stockholm – more than 250 miles away – that was threatening his home. Two hours later, he reported that the fire had been extinguished three doors down from his house. Two days after all of the details were confirmed.[133] Here was proof that this learned man hadn't suddenly gone mad or had become a religious fanatic, prone to making up the word of God.

Then a second incident happened in 1760. A widow of the recently deceased French ambassador to Sweden was given an invoice for an expensive silver set her late husband bought. She knew it had been paid for, but she couldn't find the receipt. She asked Swedenborg for help. Subsequently, she dreamed that her husband came to her and told her the exact location of the paid receipt.[134] Again, another sign for the upper classes that Swedenborg was for real, his writings were not mere ramblings, but of some consequence and that his books should be considered.

The third incident was even more dramatic and most probably caused many people to write each other, telling about what transpired and started a general swell of interest in his books. In 1761, Queen Louis Ulrika of Sweden, asked Swedenborg to relay a question to her deceased brother, Prince Augustus Wilhelm of Prussia. Three weeks later, he returned to court and whispered in her ear the answer. People heard her say that only her brother would have known what Swedenborg just told her.[135] The combination of these miraculous events promoted Swedenborg to the European world stage and prompted many learned and powerful people to read his books.

### Swedenborg's revelation

What did Swedenborg reveal? In summary, he laid out the basis of Spiritism. Although, truthfully, his books, in parts, can be hard slogging, the gems of the ideas, codified by Allan Kardec and expounded on by the books psychographed by Francisco C. Xavier are all in the eight books by Swedenborg. While, as referred to by the lecturer who mentioned Swedenborg at the start of the chapter, Swedenborg may have extrapolated certain processes of the spirit world incorrectly, his basic theme of the path to heaven lies by good works, faith, charity, and helping your neighbor, whatever your religion or lack of it, is the core of Spiritism today. He writes, in his book, *Heaven and Hell*:

> "After we die, just as soon as we arrive in the world of spirits, we are carefully sorted out by the Lord. Evil people are immediately connected with the hellish community their ruling love had affiliated them with in the world, and good people are immediately connected with the heavenly community their love and thoughtfulness and faith had affiliated them with in the world."[136]

He immediately grasped one of the central natural laws of God, that of Affiliation, where like attracts like, the law that sends our souls up or down, to be with those who we deserve to be with, according to our level of purity.

Emanuel Swedenborg made the startling claim that spirits retain their human form. At the time, the belief was divided between angels, who had wings, and demons, ugly creatures, full of bile. Emanuel wrote:

> "Years and years of daily experience have witnessed to me that after separation from the body the human spirit is a person and is in a similar form. I have seen this thousands of time, I have heard such spirits, and I have talked with them even about the fact that people in the world do not believe that they are what they are, and that scholars think people who do believe are simpletons. Spirits are heartsick over the fact that this kind of ignorance is still common in the world and especially in the church."[137]

Nothing has changed in over 260 years. Before the first sparks of the American Revolution, the eternal truths of the spirit world was laid out for human kind, then in the 1850's backed up by Allan

Kardec, and reinforced by the information in the over 400 books by Francisco C. Xavier, in the 20th century. A strikingly consistent message.

Swedenborg elaborates further; it is not just that we are in human form after death, but much more:

> "As 'spirit-people' we enjoy every outer and inner sense we enjoyed in the world. We see the way we used to, we hear and talk the way we used to; we smell and taste and feel things when we touch them the way we used to; we want, wish, crave, think, ponder, are moved, love, and intend the way we used to. Studious types still read and write as before. In a word, when we move from one life into the other, or from the one world into the other, it is like moving from (physical) place to another; and we take with us everything we owned as persons to the point that it would be unfair to say that we have lost anything of our own after death, which is only a death of the earthly body."[138]

Again, exactly according to the doctrine of Spiritism, we retain our minds, our memories and our lessons. Swedenborg's ideas made an impact upon society at that time. John Wesley, the founder of Methodist church, read Swedenborg's books and they corresponded. From the basic doctrine of Spiritism, of helping all who need assistance, regardless of their condition or religious beliefs; one can see, under the influence of Emanuel's writings, the rightness of the foundation of the Methodist church, which was established on these beliefs:

> "Methodism is characterized by its emphasis on helping the poor and the average person, it's very systematic approach to building the person, and the "church" and its missionary spirit. These ideals are put into practice by the establishment of hospitals, universities, orphanages, soup kitchens, and schools to follow Jesus's command to spread the Good News and serve all people.

> Methodists are convinced that building loving relationships with others through social service is a means of working

towards the inclusiveness of God's love. Most Methodists teach that Christ died for all of humanity, not just for a limited group, and thus everyone is entitled to God's grace. Theologically, this view is known as Arminianism, which denies that God has pre-ordained an elect number of people to eternal bliss while others perished eternally."[139]

Swedenborg first wrote to John Wesley in February, 1772, saying that the spirit world told him that Wesley wanted to speak with him. Wesley replied that he was startled, since he hadn't told anyone of his desire to talk to Swedenborg. Wesley wanted to meet with Emanuel in six months, but Swedenborg replied that it would be too late, since he would be returning to the spirit world on March 29th.[140]

A host of others, well known people, such as Ralph Waldo Emerson, Sir Arthur Conan Doyle, William Blake, Carl Jung and countless others read and were influenced by the Swedenborg's books.[141] He wrote his books knowing that they would expose him to ridicule and the danger of being labeled a heretic. Some people, during his day, considered him to be mentally ill and delusional. But, all who came in contact with him, found him to be "'kind and warm-hearted man', 'amiable in his meeting with the public', speaking 'easily and naturally of his spiritual experiences' with pleasant and interesting conversation."[142]

At his death bed, he retained his kind demeanor and his faith:

"In Swedenborg's final hours, his friend, Pastor Ferelius, told him some people thought he had written his theology just to make a name for himself and asked Swedenborg if he would like to recant. Raising himself up on his bed, his hand on his heart, Swedenborg earnestly replied,

'As truly as you see me before your eyes, so true is everything that I have written; and I could have said more had it been permitted. When you enter eternity you will see everything, and then you and I shall have much to talk about'".[143]

Swedenborg died on the date he had predicted, March 29,

1772. Four years before the start of the American Revolution, during a time of great religious and political upheavals. Momentous events, directed by the spirit world to make ready the human race for the next revelation by Allan Kardec.

# Chapter 20 - How Does Good Defeat Evil?

We have traversed the Doctrine of Spiritism and the contributors who acted as emissaries from the spirit world. The breadth and scope of the assistance from the vast spirit organization lent to us has been exposed. All of this structure, all of the Divine Natural Laws, all the work of high spirits are for what? They are for us. To take us from an embryo, who knows nothing, to an honest, upright adult. Eventually to become a valued member of the spirit community. But, how does the process work? How are the imperfections, bad habits, malicious tendencies that we see every day removed? In essence how does this all work?

How does good defeat evil? After all, if you are really good, you don't kill, go around beating up people, committing fraud and other terrible things that even good people here on earth must do on occasion to survive. So, how does the Spirit world accomplish this?

Good does defeat evil, but not in the manner that most of us think. We have been raised in the culture of the hero, who through circumstances beyond their control, uses immense power to vanquish malevolent forces. We have repeatedly viewed scenes of sword play, gun fire scattering in all directions, bodies hacked apart and blood gushing by the gallon. And this is the action of the hero, the one who saves us, mowing down and obliterating the bad guys for all eternity.

Is this what Jesus would do? Grab a high powered weapon and smite the sinful. If he did, what would our impression be of Jesus? How could that message of eternal love have shined through, when our protagonist picked up a weapon and commenced killing? It couldn't have and we all know it, but Jesus and the spirit world must overcome evil by some method? For if they were completely passive, evil would have marched like a triumphant army into heaven, their king would have been on the throne millions of years ago, not Jesus.

The answer is Jesus uses evil to defeat evil. With the help of the natural laws of God.

## Earth's Hell

According to the Spiritist doctrine, there is no permanent hell, only a place where people who have failed in the physical life go to for a period of time, until they discover the need to believe in love and begin the quest to better themselves. For after all, God is just and would not condemn a spirit for eternity, but does create the opportunity for all to rise and become pure.

The natural law of affinity, where like attracts like is the great filter that separates heaven and hell and all strata in between. *The Spirits Book* states:

*1012 second question – "Heaven" and "Hell," then, as men have imagined them, have no existence?*

"They are only symbols; there are happy and unhappy spirits everywhere. Nevertheless, as we have also told you, spirits of the same order are brought together by sympathy; but, when they are perfect, they can meet together wherever they will."[144]

Doesn't sound too bad, almost like here on earth, the riffraff gather in their seedy bars and hangouts together and only occasionally venture out in the better part of town to cause havoc. We have all known people who could live forever on the wrong side of the tracks and be perfectly happy in their existence. The law of affinity is more complex than that, "brought together" in the quote above has a hidden meaning. In the book *Liberation*, a truly frightening account of the Spirit underworld, by Andre Luiz, psychographed by Francisco C. Xavier, one of the judges in hell, Gregorio, explains his part in the greater scheme of punishment and atonement.

"The children of the Lamb may help and even rescue many. However, there are millions of individuals, like myself, who ask for neither help nor liberation. It is said that we are nothing but moral delinquents. So be it. We are criminals watching

129

over one another. The earth belongs to us because animality rules upon it, offering us the ideal atmosphere. I myself have no notion of heaven. It may be a court for the elect. But for us, the world is a vast kingdom for the condemned. In the physical body, we are prey to the web of fatal circumstances; however, the web that the lower realms have prepared for us will serve millions. If our destiny is to separate the wheat from the tares, our sifter will not lie idle. Experienced as we are in the fall, we shall test all those who appear to us on the road. The Great Judges have ordered us to guard the gates. Thus, we have servants everywhere. All men and women that have wandered away from the pathway of normal evolution are subject to us, and you surely know that there are millions of them. Furthermore, earth's tribunals are ineffective at uncovering all the crimes that occur. Yes, we are eyes in the darkness, and the smallest hidden dramas do not go unnoticed by us."[145]

Hell is organized. Hell is watching. They don't have to pull people down to their level, it all happens naturally. Lost souls descend, similar to the laws of gravity which cause us to fall to earth; selfish, materialistic, mean, avarice souls are as naturally pulled down as loving, charitable and nurturing souls are raised up. Each according to their natural selection and the power of attraction to like spirits.

Therefore, you may ask, how do these low people improve? When Andre Luiz descends into the lower regions and witnesses the lost and tortured souls residing there, he asks his instructor, Gubio, how could God allow this? Gubio supplies the answer:

"For the same instructive reasons that God does not exterminate a human nation, when, insane with a thirst for domination, it unleashes cruel and destructive wars; instead he hands it over to the expiation of its crimes and to the misfortune it has brought upon itself, so that it can learn to become part of the eternal order that presides over universal life. Over the course of many centuries, the matter used by those intelligences is worked and restructured, just like in the earthly circles; but if the Lord visits humankind by means of

130

sanctified individuals, he also corrects spirits by means of hardened or beastly ones."

"So, does that mean that evil spirits, demons…" I begin to ask hesitantly.

"… are we, ourselves." The Instructor patiently completed.[146]

Andre Luiz describes hell as if it were comparable to the "cities of the Orient two hundred years ago"[147], where carts are pulled by slaves and oxen, well dressed people, with hard sullen faces, coexisting with people in rags with misshapen features. No children to be seen. A rough, unforgiving place where the conversations were mostly about turning others into the same low state as themselves. A location, where the spirits of the living roam at night, will come to plot with others, how to cause the downfall of more spirits.

Hence, those who have been evil and now reside in hell are used to gather more of the same, in an everlasting feedback loop of accumulating similar spirits. Gubio explains to Andre Luiz, how this process functions on an individual basis:

"Yes, Andre, each mind lives amongst the company it has chosen. The same principle applies for those who live within the dense body or outside of it. It is important to realize, however, that most of the souls in this place are here due to the forces of attraction. They were incapable of perceiving the presence of spirit benefactors who work with among incarnates in endeavors of self-denial and benevolence, and due to their low vibrational level resulting from repeated wrongs, impenitent idleness, or willful crystallization in error, they found nothing but darkness all around them. Alone and confused, they went looking for discarnates with whom that had an affinity and they naturally met in this immense hive carrying the whole load of the destructive passions that characterized their journey. When such souls get here, however, they must endure the watchfulness of the powerful and hardened intelligences who rule like dictators in these regions, where the bitter fruits of evil and indifference fill the storehouse of unprepared and malicious hearts."[148]

Therefore, the wicked amongst us are placed in a truly evil realm, where they can determine, over the course of time, if this is where they wish to spend the rest of their days. After all, what could be a more direct application of one of the main doctrines of Spiritism; do unto others as you would have them do unto you. This is precisely what is occurring to the spirits that have committed sins in their physical life, others are doing unto them what they have done unto others, and by the way, how does it feel?

## Path to Redemption

The souls of hell are not abandoned. Gubio explains, "The same law of self-effort applies here as well."[149] Hence, each individual spirit must arrive at a watershed moment to decide from then on, to pursue a better life, a life driven by selflessness and love opposed to materialism and hate.

The team led by Gubio, in which Andre Luiz is a member, has a mission to save a particular spirit. As a byproduct to the mission, the team assists one of Judge Gregorio's henchman, Saldanha, to seek a better life and flee from the confines of hell. Others from hell find out and come to the team seeking a new path. One poor spirit pleads for a way out of the evil environment in which he is forced to reside.

> "Please, save me from the cruel judges! I can't stand the atrocities I'm forced to commit anymore. I've heard that Saldanha himself has been transformed. I can't persist in error any longer! I'm afraid that Gregorio will come after me, but even if I have to endure that most dreadful pain, I'll face it head-on. I would rather suffer his blows than go back. Please, help me! I yearn for a new course, one that will lead me to the Good."[150]

Little did that poor spirit realize, that his own thoughts originally threw him into the pit. Furthermore, this act of immersion into the vat of evil, the constant source of emotional pain was the cure precisely prescribed for him by the natural laws of God. Where he could suffer what he has wrought. Feeling the damage that he has delivered to others, which slowly started the spark that led him to the realization that there must be a better alternative.

How many of us, in some distant past life, has spent time in that horrible place. Learning lessons that permeated our soul. Teachings that we swore we would never forget, but upon the next reincarnation, sliding back into old habits. The quest for perfection is not a straight line, but a winding road, gathering understanding and awareness along the way. Sometimes we fail and other times make great progress.

Therefore, we are expected to make our best efforts to pick ourselves up. God only allows us a short time for childhood in each life, where we can be molded, and allowed the chance to layer better morals upon our spirit, in an unquestioning manner. We are not spoon feed easy answers; God does not come down from heaven and scream at us, why in the heck are you doing this? Don't you know you shall pay for everything that you do while on earth? That would be as if we gave students the correct answers to every test. The students would all have "A's", but be no smarter, no wiser about how to think and behave. Growth must be from within. Understanding this, brings comprehension to the entire scheme of the spirit world. The place for hell and the place for heaven; the reason for the eternal toil for perfection.

# Chapter 21 - How the Spirit World Guides the Destiny of the Earth and the Human Race

The process for transforming primitive souls to pure spirits has been explored. The spirit world doesn't just focus on us individually. An entire planet must be guided to construct the platform to enable the collective human race to participate in the trials needed at the right time.

Beginning in the remotest ages with primitive tribes there has been a recurring theme of our destiny being guided by supreme powers. The Old and New Testaments actually tell of events being managed by God. Allan Kardec published *The Spirits Book* which for the first time revealed the extent the Hand of God plays into our past, present, and future activities. The books psychographed by Francisco C. Xavier expose some of the exact processes by which we are directed.

This chapter collects together and describes the tools by which the spirit world pushes and pulls the levers and sets the dials to manipulate the human race to achieve their desired results.

Throughout recorded history mankind has consulted the gods (as known by them) for direction. The Greeks had the Oracle of Delphi, the Romans had the Sibylline Books, and the Chinese had the I Ching, which is still being used by many today. The major religions each have their holy works, Christians have the *Bible*, Islam has the *Koran*, Hinduism has the *Bhagavad Gita*, Baha'i's have their books, such as *The Seven Valleys*; all speak of an end times, a period of a termination for some and a new beginning for others. All texts imply a direct involvement of a higher world into our affairs or at the very least a power which has the ability to know the future.

## The Objective of the Spirit World

While, all of us desire to know our personal destinies,

somehow we believe that foreknowledge of events will make us better prepared and less anxious, at times we ponder larger horizons, what is the future for the human race? What is the endgame for us here on earth? For Christians the answer is the Apocalypse, the final judgment of us all by Jesus, as recorded in the Bible; "Now when the Son of Man comes in his majesty, accompanied by all the angels, he will sit on the throne of his glory. And all the nations will be gathered before him and he will separate some from the others as a shepherd separates the sheep from the goats, and he will put the sheep on his right and the goats on his left. Then, the King will say to those on his right, 'Come, you who are blessed by my Father'".[151]

We are being told in the New Testament that a great division will be coming. According to Spiritism, we are being prepared for the transition of the earth from an expiratory sphere to a higher level, where the good spirits are the majority of the planet. Allan Kardec, in his book *Genesis*, explains the implications of the final judgment, "Since the good must finally reign on the earth, it will be necessary to exclude spirits who are hardened in evil and who could bring trouble to it. God has already allowed them the time needed for their improvement; but when the time comes in which, through the moral progress of its inhabitants, the earth must ascend in the hierarchy of worlds, it will be off limits as a home for incarnates and discarnates who have not taken advantage of the teachings they have been in a position to receive there. They will be exiled to lowers worlds as formerly those of the Adamic races were exiled to the earth, and they will be replaced by better spirits".[152]

The weeding out of the reluctant spirits and the populating of the planet with good spirits will be a gradual conversion. We are being groomed to attain the state required for us to inhabit a non-expiratory world. In *Genesis*, the Apocalypse will not occur in a big bang but will be; "According to the Spirits the earth will not be transformed by a cataclysm that will suddenly wipe out an entire generation. The current generation will disappear gradually and the new one will follow it in the same way, without there have been any change in the natural order of things".[153]

Therefore, the process is and was happening all around us and is continual, from the first human discovering fire to the small gatherings of Spiritists. It is in God's design that this conversion occurs. And again in *Genesis*, according to the Spirit world; "When something is in God's designs, it must be accomplished one way or another. Men and women contribute to its execution, but no one is indispensable; otherwise, God would be at the mercy of God's creatures".[154]

How does the spirit world march us inexorably toward their goal? As we all know, the human race are undisciplined soldiers, we seldom are able to parade in lockstep, without plenty of training and threats of punishment. The answer is that there is an active campaign being waged. Battles are being fought with knowledge, fraternity and persuasion. Armies are being mobilized and troops sent to various locations. The human race is in constant conflict with the spirit world and we don't even realize it. We are pushing for greater power and materialism, while the spirit realm is countering with education and love.

## The Campaign of the Spirit World

A cynic would cry out, "No contest!" to the fight against materialism, given our current culture. The battle for changing behavior from idolizing the latest tennis shoe or beauty product to emphasizing charity and good works seems like a lost cause. Most of us look at the present world and are unable to determine the required tactics to win this contest. Which bring us to the overwhelming advantage of the spirit world:

"Amateurs talk Strategy and Professionals talk Logistics", quote attributed to General Omar Bradley (US general in World War II).

Logistics, the organization of complex tasks, the spirit world's ability to move souls, and not just any spirits, but those with specific skills, to vital points at the correct time is the key. The spirit world is able flood any contested field with their soldiers. Yes, the troops are human and prone to failure, but as written in *Genesis*; "If those entrusted with a mission fail to fulfill it, someone else will be assigned to it. No mission is unavoidable; individuals are always free to fulfill that which has been entrusted to them and which they have voluntarily accepted. If they do not fulfill it, they lose the benefit and assume responsibility for the delays that might results from their negligence or ill will. If they become an obstacle to its fulfillment, God can snap them with one breath".[155]

How will we achieve an even balance between our religious life, scientific advancements, and public good and private responsibility? There is a plan and it has been in progress for thousands of years. It is a design of slow and deliberate movements of souls in the right place at the right time. Always with the objective to raise the human race's maturity, knowledge, and spirituality little by little. Sometimes with seemingly great leaps backwards, but always in the end a little progress is apparent. The first mention of the existence of a plan, with Jesus leading the effort is in the Holy Bible; "God has now revealed to us his mysterious plan regarding Christ, a plan to fulfill his own good pleasure. And this is the plan: At the right time he will bring everything together under the authority of Christ – everything in heaven and earth. Furthermore, because we are united with Christ, we have received an inheritance from God, for he chose us in advance, and he makes everything work out according to his plan".[156]

Paul himself knew he was part of the plan, for he wrote, "But even before I was born, God chose me and called me by his marvelous grace. Then it please him to reveal his son to me so that I would proclaim the Good News about Jesus to the Gentiles".[157]

In the book, *On the Way to the Light*, the spirit Emmanuel, writes that the Apostles of Jesus, while high order spirits on a mission, lacked the ability to resist the impulse to create an aristocratic character to the new churches, an aspect that attempted to retain the elitism found in Judaism. Something had to be done, therefore Emmanuel reports, "Thus, Jesus decided to call upon the luminous and energetic spirit of Paul of Tarsus to help carry out his ministry. This decision was one of the most significant events in the history of Christianity. The deeds and letters of Paul became a powerful universalizing element for the new doctrine".[158]

Paul writes that he was chosen for his mission before he was born, but Emmanuel reports that Paul was used because the circumstances demanded it. This illustrates the depth of the planning by the spirit world, spirits are put into place to act as back-ups in case the original people either fail their mission or need assistance. Another example of the multi-layered plan to move us toward enlightenment is the preparation for the arrival of Allan Kardec. We tend to think of Allan Kardec as being in a vacuum, a wonderful person who had the idea of organizing the communications of the spirit world in a form we could all read and use for our personal instruction. In fact, Allan Kardec was just one part of the overall plan, as described by Emmanuel, "On his mission of enlightenment and consolation, however, Allan Kardec would be accompanied by a plethora of companions and collaborators, whose regenerative work would manifest not only in matters of a doctrinal nature, but in every area of intellectual activity of the 19th century. Science in those days made large strides that would lead it to the heights of the 20th century".[159]

This demonstrates the complexity of the resources the Spirit world possesses and the intricate planning that must have been accomplished. They are able to mobilize spirits to be reincarnated in selected fields, whether as scientists, professors, philosophers, mediums or politicians, to actively promote their objectives. Imagine the complexity of ensuring the correct families, with the right beliefs and attitudes, wealth and connections, to procreate and raise the children who grew up to change the world. Think of the variables, with the great number of diseases that were incurable in the 1800's, the rate of infant mortality, temptations for those with money and power, the list could go on and on. It is as if the spirit world ran impossibly complex Monte Carlo simulations (an algorithm that runs a simulation numerous times taking into account changing variables[160]). Truly, it is exciting to imagine how the strategy and logistics are actually taking place.

# The Campaign – The Big Picture

The spirit world's design for our ascension to a higher world does not only encompass strategies for our personal, spiritual and educational growth, but the structure, organization, and boundaries of countries. For a large group of individuals to gain enlightenment the right surroundings must be created. The environment must set so people are able to begin the steps toward the true path. They need to be able to not worry about where their next meal is coming from, or if their city will be attacked at any moment, or if their dictator will suddenly decide that someone must die.

The rise of Greece and their experiments in democracy, individualism and philosophy were not accidents. The spirit world wished to divorce mankind from their primitive attachments to tribal leaders and kings, superstitions and magic talismans, to a higher level of comprehending the world around them. Therefore, according to Emmanuel, the spirit world, "Under the influence of the merciful soul of the Christ, all Greece was peopled with eminent artists and thinkers in the areas of philosophy and science. The Italic and Eleatic schools let the way with the fervent idealism of Pythagoras and Xenophanes".[161]

Here is a case study of the spirit world deliberately populating a specific area of the world with spirits chosen for their required skills. The aim of the exercise was to effect a revolutionary change in the social and intellectual structure of an entire people.

On the other hand, when the spirit world's plan for a society went astray, through the collective failures of their messengers while incarnated, they could pull the plug on the experiment and use the pieces later for a new attempt. An example of this is the destruction of Rome, as described by Emmanuel, "Jesus ordered the transformation of the organized and powerful Empire. Its proud eagles had sailed all the seas; the Mediterranean was its property and all peoples had kneeled down in homage and obedience; but an invisible force snatched away its diadems, took away its strength and reduced its glory to a pile of ashes".[162]

The spirit realm regrouped and analyzed new pathways to achieve their objective. Like any good craftsman, the spirit world takes care of its tools, the lives led in the Greek and Roman worlds would be used to reshape Europe. Using these veteran resources, Emmanuel reports on the new plan that took shape a hundred years after Christ's arrival on earth, "A few years before the end of the first century after the coming of the new doctrine the powers of the spirit world made an analysis of the dreadful situation of the world in view of the future. Under Jesus' direction, they established new lines of progress for civilization, marking the initial characteristics of modern day European countries".[163]

The spirit world was embarking on setting the stage for the rebirth of Western Civilization, a resurgence that would take it further than the boundaries of the Mediterranean, to influence the entire world. Thirteen hundred years later one could detect the slow transformation of Europe climbing out of the Dark Ages into the beginnings of the Renaissance and the Age of Discovery, which would be the foundation of our modern world. As recorded by Emmanuel, the detailed plans for the Renaissance were as follows:

"On the Iberian Peninsula, under the guidance of Henry of Sagres (Henry the Navigator), who was responsible for great and beneficial accomplishments, schools were founded for navigators to sail the seas in search of unknown lands. Numerous precursors to the Reformation appeared everywhere, fighting against abuses of a religious nature. Former masters of Athens reincarnated in Italy to spread the most beautiful jewels of genius and sentiment in the areas of painting and sculpture. England and France prepared for the great democratic mission that Christ would entrust to them. Commerce spread from the restricted waters of the Mediterranean to the great waves of the Atlantic in search of forgotten roads to the East. Jesus guided this rebirth of all human activities, which would define the positions of the various European countries, and invested each one with a particular responsibility in the structure of the planet's collective evolution".[164]

140

Whereas, we on earth believe we are exceptional when our countries or corporations make five-year plans, the plans of the spirit world span hundreds if not thousands of years. The spirit world sets general and broad objectives and constantly monitors progress and results. The outcomes of each attempt to guide us are measured and modifications to the overall design are made to maintain the forward progress to the overall goal. And the ultimate goal is to prepare our world to shed its primitive reason for being, that of a place to learn the basic lessons of fraternity and pay off our sins, to one where spirits come to toil mainly to expand their learning and continue to grow toward a higher level.

## The Campaign – In the Trenches

Given how the broad strategy is set, updated, measured and new plans generated, the question remains about the performance of the spirits on the ground, fulfilling their missions to achieve their targeted objectives. As with any army, the organization in the field is meant to make the most efficient use of resources at hand as possible. In the writings by the spirit authors, four major categories of on the ground forces are found.

1. Missions by high order/ pure spirits.

2. Outposts on earth of the Spirit world.

3. Missions performed by regular spirits (on the level of Nossa Lar).

4. Missions performed by veteran spirits who have been successful in past missions.

## 1 - Missions by High Order Spirits

The missions by high order or pure spirits are high impact and high visibility, they are meant to cause significant changes in our growth. One striking example of a mission by a high order spirit is that of Charlemagne. Emmanuel describes the necessity of bringing organization back to Western Europe after the fall of Rome. Given the splitting of the Roman Empire into many weak states, they were not in a position to resist the threat of Islamic invasion, during its dramatic years of conquest. Therefore, Emmanuel reports:

"It is after this period that Jesus allowed the reincarnation of one of the most upstanding Roman emperors, who was eager to help the European spirit in its bitter decadence. This spirit was reborn as Charlemagne, the true organizer of the scattered elements needed to found the western world. Nearly illiterate, he created the greatest traditions of strength and goodness, with the loftiness that characterized his balanced and highly evolved spirit. During his 46-year reign, Charlemagne promoted education and corrected the administrative defects rampant among the disorganized peoples of Europe, thereby leaving wonderful prospects for Latinism".[165]

Not only did the spirit world intervene to guide countries, but also to lead organized religions to a better path. During the years of the Catholic Inquisition, that appalling institution, that tortured innocents for their beliefs, if they did not prostate themselves before the dogma of the Church, the spirit world determined the Catholic Church needed to be reminded of the true reason for their existence. Emmanuel writes about the lesson the Spirit world gave to the priesthood:

"To that end, one of Jesus' greatest apostles reincarnated as Francis of Assisi. His great and luminous spirit shone near Rome in the region of desolate Umbria. His reformist activity took place without the sparring over words per se, because his priesthood was an example lived out in poverty and complete humility. Even so, the Church failed to grasp the fact that his lesson was meant for it, and once more refused a gift from Jesus".[166]

The planned growth of the human race not only included our political and religious spheres, but that of philosophy and science. Spiritism has spoken of a time when science would prove the basic tenets of our doctrine. To this end the Spirit world introduced a great leap forward during the 1700's, as described by Emmanuel:

"The 18th century began with equally renewing struggles, but high order spirits of Philosophy and Science – who reincarnated chiefly in France – would fight against the errors of society and politics, upending the principles of divine right, in whose name all sorts of barbarities were being committed. Amongst this plethora of reformers were the venerable figures of Voltaire, Montesquieu, Rousseau, D'Alembert, Diderot and Quesnay. Their benevolent teachings reverberated in the future United States and throughout the rest of the world".[167]

As one can see, many of the people in our history books have been deliberately planted in our midst to help us improve our world. Their appearance was not mere chance, but a task executed according to a plan. A plan that culminates in our planet evolving to a level where we all would love to live.

## 2 – Outposts on Earth

Outposts, a place of protection and sustenance, a sanctuary where good spirits can rest and plan. All of these are required to support the missions of a multitude of discarnate and incarnated spirits. In several books influenced by the spirit Andre Luiz, as he embarks on training and educational missions to the earth, the base of operations is usually a Spiritual Center. The centers are used for multiple purposes, for spreading the doctrine of Spiritism, helping incarnated and disincarnated souls, and as a protected meeting place for teams of workers from the Spirit world to discuss plans and progress and to receive orders for their next assignment.

In the book *Action and Reaction*, Andre Luiz is told about the need for security within the centers, he notices the center is surrounded by misshapen lost spirits and wonders why they can't be allowed inside for their needed comfort:

"Your suggestion would certainly be the ideal solution. However, only those who can bear its light with due respect can enter the sacred room. Almost all the brothers and sisters in the square exhibit disfigurement caused by their perversity, or they harbor fierce sentiments that their moving prayers fail to hide. With such dispositions they cannot bear the impact of the light inside because it is made up of special photons characterized by a particular electromagnetic content that is indispensable for the institute's security. Many of these disturbed brothers and sisters may be clamoring with their lips that they long for the benefits of prayer inside the sanctuary, but in reality, once there they would love to trample the sublime name of our Heavenly Father in a display of sarcasm and blasphemy. So, in order to keep them from disturbing the divine atmosphere that we must provide for pure and comforting prayer, our guides have ordered us to keep the light gradated against easily avoidable disturbance and harm".[168]

Therefore, a Spiritist sanctuary must above all else be a safe place for both incarnates and discarnates to meet and work. Without the correct environment, trying to assist truly ready souls would be made most difficult when surrounded by hostile spectators. Spiritists and those who are interested require an elevated environment to pray and meditate. Mediums certainly require a space for the good spirits to conjugate so they may be allowed to send their messages to the living. Andre Luiz discusses one such sanctuary with a spirit who is working at the center, "The majority of needy individuals came into contact with Jesus through a humble bowl of soup or a sheltering roof. Washing lepers, healing the insane or assisting orphans and the forsaken elderly, Christ's followers created work for themselves and dedicated themselves to unfortunate souls, enlightening their minds and offering lessons of substantial interest to laymen of the living faith. As you can see, we are making evangelical Spiritism the recapitulation of early Christianity".[169]

There are some centers that do not concentrate on the living, but rather the poor souls trapped on earth. In one such center in Rio, Andre notices the center caters mostly to orphaned children. Very few adult incarnates, he asks his team leader why this is so; "We avail ourselves of the center – regarded reverently for its principles of Christian solidarity – as a place for spreading healthy ideas. The foundation concentrates much more on souls than physical bodies, much more on eternal thoughts than on transitory matters".[170]

144

Therefore, Spiritual centers are also important to assist the lost souls still trapped on earth. Souls, who may one day raise themselves into a better state, to supply one more spirit to assist the people of earth to promote the status of the planet. The basic math of the battle for earth is; one more spirit who wishes to attain a purer state supplies one more soldier in the battle to transform the earth. Eventually, numbers will win out. As more souls are influenced by Spiritism, the culture on earth gradually transforms to conform to our doctrines, then when spirits that have been influenced by the Spiritist centers on earth reincarnate, they find the environment to have altered and being human, they tend to follow the general direction of society. The same idea of a gradual transformation is presented in Allan Kardec's *Genesis*:

"Disbelievers, fanatics, and absolutists consequently will be able to return with *inborn* ideas of faith, tolerance and liberty. Upon their return they will find that things have changed and will experience the influence of the new environment into which they have been born. Instead of opposing new ideas, they will support them".[171]

Spiritist centers are a vital link in the organization of the spirit world. They are where the encounter for people's beliefs are being fought. The only battlefield that is advantageous territory, away the clamoring culture of today's materialism and separated from lower spirits with bad intentions.

### 3 – Missions Performed by Regular Spirits

What about the normal foot soldier who is striving to actively assist the progress of human kind? The assignments given to spirits vary widely from raising and guiding children to work in a Spiritual Center as a medium. In the book, *The Messengers*, Andre Luiz learns about the importance of the missions that are meant to foster the spread of Spiritism on earth. Andre is curious about the success rate of the missions, he speaks with a knowledgeable person who explains the problems associated with their tasks, "Any constructive task has difficulties, barriers to be overcome. Very few workers have the willpower to fight the battles inherent in the challenge. An enormous percentage will balk at the first firewall they encounter and will retreat when the opportunities become threatening".[172]

"An enormous percentage", is a startling statement. This serves to disabuse ourselves of the belief of the smooth inevitable march to a higher plane. The war in the trenches is hard fought and is met with failure more often than success. One example of a failed mission is described by Octavio, a person that regretfully explains his failed mission to Andre:

"After having acquired great debts by committing crimes and injustices on Earth in former lifetimes, I eventually found my way to Nossa Lar and was helped by wonderful, tireless friends. In order to eventually return to Earth with a mission of service in the area of extrasensory communication, I underwent an intense thirty-year preparation. I was eager to pay off my debts and make something good out of myself. I could count on so much help! The Ministry of Communication gave me all the assistance and guidance it could; in addition, six friends also helped me immensely. Technicians from the Ministry of Assistance went with me to Earth and helped in my transition process. My life, exercising my well-developed mediumistic capabilities, was to make me part of a great team of spirit workers assigned to Brazil. Marriage was not in my program; not because the duties of a husband could be incompatible with those of a medium, but because, for my particular case, it was deemed advisable to exclude it".[173]

Octavio speaks about preparing for his mission for thirty years. The spirit world invested a great deal in Octavio, much more than is spent training people on earth for even the most complex tasks. Octavio goes on to describe that he had a wonderful mother who brought him up in the Spiritist doctrine, while his father was a more materialistic, but still a good person. Octavio lost his mother at fifteen and his father re-married. His step-mother had three children and his father and step-mother together had three more. They were the six friends who had assisted him in the spirit world. Octavio was to nurture the small children after his father passed away. Octavio continues his story detailing how he treated his step-mother, who was always good to Octavio, "Not having anyone to turn to, she asked me for help again and again – and to my shame, I ignored her. Two years after my father's death, my stepmother, was diagnosed with a devastating skin illness and was confined to a clinic. By this time, my heartlessness had reached such a level that I was totally disgusted by her and the kids, and just walked away from it all – not realizing that I was abandoning my six best friends from Nosso Lar to an uncertain fate".[174]

Not only did Octavio fail individually, but he certainly must have adversely affected the mission of his six friends. This is just one of the many examples of failure in *The Messengers*. Octavio is just one of many sent on missions, again in the book *The Messengers*, we learn from a trusted source:

"Since the very beginning of the spread of the Spiritist precepts on Earth, Nosso Lar has sent teams to the planet with the job of teaching moral values. Hundreds of workers leave here annually with the goal of helping others and making amends for their past faults. But this has not brought about the desired results. A few have achieved some success, but the majority of workers have failed altogether. We have provided assistance on numerous occasions, but have seen little success. Very few achieve their goal in the arduous realms of mediumship and spiritual teaching".[175]

Failures for individuals had many causes, pride, quest for material goods, bad marriages, sexual temptations and others factors that daily affect our lives and lead us to different choices. Not only do the reincarnated spirits have to contend with their own human weaknesses, but there are also hurdles to those who are actively striving to spread Spiritism. Andre Luiz was told, "Did you think that spiritual evolution would be left to automatic mechanisms? On earth, our perception of spiritual matters often become warped by the dogmatism of organized religions and their conventional displays of faith".[176]

Andre is being told two distinct concepts. One is that our

147

spiritual evolutionary path is not one solely based on our progress and introspections at a pace determined by our collective advances, but in reality is a campaign to spur us on. To get us out of the materialistic mire and onto a more balanced existence. The other concept is the resistance to change that is presented by organized religions. Andre is told of the problems that exists to stop or dull the advance of Spiritism, "The Catholic Church classifies our work as diabolic, while the Protestant churches block our efforts to help those who long to know more of the eternal truths".[177]

The most important fact to remember is the battle to spread Spiritism is extremely young, barely over 150 years. A mere moment of time in the vast history of our race. Even failure brings about the seeds of success. When a spirit is reincarnated and fails their mission, they gather valuable experience, the same as any person who first tries to learn a job. The primary attempt is always a learning episode. Given that our soldiers are immortal, they have the ability to return to the battle, with more skills, knowledge and greater determination to thrive the next time. Which brings us to the next category, missions performed by veteran spirits.

## 4 – Missions Performed by Veteran Spirits

As in every organization, special considerations and respect is given to those who have demonstrated their abilities. Management understands very well that the success of their plans usually rests on key individuals, people who have passed trials before and are loyal workers that can be depended upon to achieve the targets that were set. Additionally, feedback from these key personnel are carefully analyzed, for they are on the field and have the most valuable intelligence about the circumstances in which they operate. Plans will be changed as the superiors in charge learn and assess valuable information given to them by their trusted lieutenants.

An illustration of the dynamic modifications of plans is given by Andre Luiz in the book *Workers of the Life Eternal*. Andre Luiz and the team he was part of, were preparing to assist an older woman to leave the earthly world, when they were told of an urgent requirement. Instead of helping the woman leave her physical life, they would provide her strength to continue on for some time. Andre, used to static plans, was curious about this event. His superior, Jeronimo, answered his question:

"The measure should not cause any surprise. No one, other than God has supreme power. All of us, when performing the tasks entrusted to our responsibility, will experience limitations or an increase of duties according to superior purposes. The future can be calculated along general lines, but we are unable to predetermine anything with regards to the area of divine interference. The Father carries out the organization of the universe with unlimited independence in the area of Infallible Wisdom. We cooperate with a certain amount of freedom in tasks on our world, and are subject to necessary and enlightening interdependence due to our own individual imperfections. God knows, while we cannot even come close to know".[178]

Therefore, the team based out of Nosso Lar, is part of the process to carry out the predetermine course of lives, but sometimes they will receive contradictory orders from a higher sphere. This points to the possibility that their plans are remotely supervised and when information is received that affect the milestones given, alterations will descend from on high.

The team performs their new duties, which now involves keeping a frail lady, named Albina, alive for a longer time than originally planned. She was a key person in the formation of a Spiritist Center. Albina has a daughter named Loide, who is expecting a baby girl. Andre Luiz observes Albina's students and her family praying for her and questions whether their prayers could be the cause of the adjustment of her intended life span. The answer is no, they are not the reason.

Next, Andre sees a small boy of about eight years old, coming in to see his grandmother. Andre is told, the boy (nicknamed Joaozinho) is the reason for the prolonged life of Albina. Jeronimo tells Andre, "He is not Albina's blood grandson, although he considers himself to be. He was an orphan who was left on her doorstep after he was born. Loide has been looking after him at her house ever since Albina became bedridden. In spite of the ordeal, Joaozinho is a noble and unselfish servant of Jesus, and has reincarnated on an evangelical mission. He has extensive credit from the past. He has been connected to Albina's family for a few centuries, and he has returned to the bosom of dearly loved individuals on his way to future apostolic service".[179]

Andre is now extremely curious how this boy could change a person's fate. He learns that the baby girl Albina's daughter is carrying is intended to be the boy's wife. The boy, Joaozinho, was worried that the untimely death of his grandmother could affect his wife-to-be's birth. Therefore, he asked for a postponement of her death until after Loide, his future mother-in-law, could give birth. Andre is informed about the boy and his intended bride, "They are not purified redeemed spirits, but rather valuable workers with sufficient moral credit to obtain more important opportunities. Despite still being a child, and due to his rich insight outside the physical realm, this reincarnate servant has been forewarned about the imminent death of our venerable sister".[180]

Andre then learns more about how the seemingly small innocent child changed an old lady's date of death; "So he asked for the help of all intercessory channels during the moments in which his lucid soul was able to operate outside his material body, and through his insistent pleas, he succeeded in obtaining a short postponement of Albina's discarnation".[181]

One can see how qualified workers, those who have past proven performances, are able through their accumulated experiences to understand what groups to notify about shifting circumstances and how to communicate their vital information, in order to modify plans for a better chance of attainment on the ground. The number of tested veterans will grow over time. Allowing for more missions and an increased percentage of successful operations. The campaign for our spiritual enlightenment is dependent on seasoned people, like Joaozinho and his bride-to-be. By the efforts of these veterans, those of us who are embarking on missions for the first time will learn and be guided to eventual triumph. It may take several reincarnations to become an effective team member, but all who strive in the service of our Lord, will one day be victorious.

## Conclusion

The endgame for our elevation as a non-expiratory world started with Allan Kardec. By the middle 1800's, the spirit world had set the basic boundaries of Europe, started the rise of the Americas, and began the industrial revolution. Alongside all these accomplishments, the great advancements of science began to appear. The last phase of the campaign has been in progress for over 150 years. Western Civilization has been formed into the shape it is today, to begin receiving in earnest the doctrines laid out by Allen Kardec. While at times, the current state of Western Civilization seems too materialistic, too weak to confront the enemies who wish to completely tear down our freedoms, and too corrupt to ever evolve into an society governed by honest politicians, we must see how far we have come since the days when Christians were devoured by lions for the amusement of the Roman masses, and have faith that our destiny is being guided to a wonderful conclusion. An ending which is described in *The Spirits Book*:

*1019. "Will the reign of goodness ever be established upon the earth?"*

"Good will reign upon the earth when, among the spirits who come to dwell in it, the good shall be more numerous that the bad; for they will then bring in the reign of love and justice, which are the source of good and of happiness. It is through moral progress and practical conformity with the laws of God, that men will attract to the earth good spirits, who will keep bad ones away from it; but the latter will not definitively quit the earth until its people shall be completely purified from pride and selfishness"

...

"Devote yourselves, then, with zeal and courage to the great work of regeneration, all you who are possessed of faith and good will; you will reap a hundredfold for all the seed you sow. Woe to those who close their eyes against the light; for they will have condemned themselves to long ages of darkness and sorrow! Woe to those who center their enjoyment in the pleasures of the earthly life; for they will undergo privations more numerous than their present pleasures! And woe, above all, to the selfish; for they will find none to aid them in bearing the burden of their future misery!"[182]

Since we are not there yet, we still have plenty of work to do. We must work for the future of the entire human race. We should be content with winning the little battles, over ourselves first and foremost, then others. Demonstrating by example and teaching when invited the precepts of Spiritism. Andre Luiz, after visiting a spiritual center in Rio de Janeiro voiced the same conclusion; "I realized that, above any type of individualistic concern, the spreading of spiritual light across the earth is not a miraculous event, but rather patient and gradual edification".[183]

# Chapter 22 - ADC – After Death Communication – David G.

David G. had an After Death Communication (ADC) experience which illustrates how the spirit world communicates with us and the power they have to speak directly to our minds. I take the reader through David's experiences and relate what the spirit world is actually doing.

David G. had an experience that changed his life. He started communicating with a deceased niece at her funeral. You can read his whole story at the NDERF.org website.

On the day his niece died in a car accident, David felt strange, like someone wanted to talk with him. He felt guilt playing golf on that day, but he felt his niece, Michelle, telling him it was alright. On the day of the funeral he described what happened:

"Two days later, the day of her Catholic wake, at the evening session, I had a sudden and undeniable verbal communication from Michelle. I was sitting with my wife in the second row at the funeral home before her casket. She said in the voice of a four year old, "Here comes trouble" and communicated without words that I should go out to the parking lot to meet with a young man who had just arrived. I could clearly see him distraught and teary-eyed with a small group of other young people her age in the parking lot though there was no window in the room. Over and over she wanted me to go out to him and I refused with my rational mind. There were no words at first other than "Here comes trouble" and "Go see him, Uncle Dave". I just knew I should go and I clearly saw the scene in my mind, the same way I was hearing her words. I sobbed heavily, overcome with a feeling of... awe? emotion? it's hard to say. I was just hearing her voice so clearly and seeing what was going on in a place I couldn't physically see. I just 'knew' what was happening, and where the boy was. I didn't know who he was, only that she said "Here comes trouble". I knew her boyfriend at the time, I had met him at the house. He was in the room in the funeral home with us. This was someone else. I didn't know who he was, I just knew he was there and that she wanted me to go to him.

After I delayed long enough (perhaps a few minutes?) there was no longer a need to go outside. The moment had passed and I felt it. I could see him leaving some of the friends, and moving with others toward the door of the funeral home and eventually into the long hallway crowded with mourners of all ages. It would be a while before he entered the room where I was with my wife and her family. As a part of me followed his slow walk toward the room, I continued the communication with my niece Michelle. She spoke so clearly, in a young voice I best remember.

I asked her where she was and why she was talking to me. She told me that she wasn't speaking to me directly, but that I alone had heard. She said it was a matter of openness to the experience. I asked her why her voice was that of a four year old. She said there was no actual voice, that she and I were sharing thoughts - thought energies? - and that my mind was putting a voice onto what was being communicated. She deliberately said in her young voice "I could sound like this", then in her 19 year old voice "Or like this", then in the voice of a 64 year old woman she would never be "Or like this". Each time my mind heard the voice clearly and knew what I was hearing. It was indeed my mind putting an audible voice on some other way of communicating. I just 'knew' it. It's so hard to put into words what I was experiencing." [184]

This episode perfectly illustrates the communication between the spirit world and the physical world. Spiritism tells us that we all have the capacity to be mediums, to somehow communicate with discarnates (people who are no longer living on the physical plane). But, of course, some of us are better and more adept than others. David G. has that ability, since his niece told him that she was directing her thoughts to everyone in the funeral hall.

Spirits talk directly to us, by radiating their thoughts to our

154

Cerebral center, which controls senses, sight, hearing, touch and our psychic abilities. Thoughts are real in the spiritual world, as in here on earth, they are the beginning of any actions, but more so in Michelle's new location. By finding a receptor, Michelle could by thought alone, talk to David in whatever voice she so desired.

There are two more details I would like to add. The first is that most certainly, Michelle was not alone in the funeral hall; there must have been other spirits there to help her control her thoughts and emotions after such a violent death. Secondly, Michelle must have been an advanced spirit, for most people when they die, go through a, at least, several day period where they are confused or even not aware they have died. Therefore, for Michelle to have communicated so calmly and with clarity reveals her to be well acquainted with the spirit world and that upon her death, she realized she had accomplished her mission on earth.

Next David G. learns more from Michelle's side, the other world, as the Druids called it:

"I asked again, or for the first time, where she was and I saw a blackness, a void, in which there was a spinning orb about ten feet tall to my perception. The spinning orb was the earth and it was spinning very fast - many revolutions per second. Two spiritual forms approached the spinning orb/earth. The spiritual forms I mention were to my perception some sort of misty beings - ghostlike - with some semblance of humanoid scale and size, and yet they were formless. They were human size only in reference to my point of reference, the reference in which the rapidly spinning earth was about ten feet in diameter. As one being said some sort of farewell to the other, the other lifted up in a large puff and disappeared as a funnel shaped mist onto the surface of the planet. In a matter of seconds it reappeared, this time as a small point of a funnel shaped mist lifting up and coming back to the same size and general shape it had before. It walked / drifted away with the first being as they discussed what had happened during that lifetime. I knew I had witnessed a human lifetime from another perspective, a spiritual form experiencing a single human lifetime and then coming back to review it with a friend/peer. It's hard to explain but it was so clear to me.

I also saw/felt/experienced total darkness that wasn't darkness, a void that wasn't a void but was everything and everywhere all at once. No time, no space. In that absence of anything I could be anywhere at anytime just by thinking about it. All I had to do was to have a thought and I was there. Everywhere all at once. It was the most amazing, profound, deep experience I have ever had in this human lifetime. (Later that day and for days after this whole experience I journaled the whole thing extensively. I haven't re-read the journal but I have it in my possession to this day.)

I believe she also shared the moment of her death during that time we were speaking. She also communicated to me that I shouldn't share this experience with her immediate family as she came from a troubled family with a horribly abusive childhood. They wouldn't understand at this time, nor should that abusive energy be part of the equation at that time. I honored her wishes."[185]

David G. saw the spiritual world from Michelle's perspective and he saw her judgment after she died. For a moment he too existed in the other dimension, where time and space is altered, and all exists in a world of vibrations, where our minds control the energy around us. Energy to make us look that way we desire, energy to have us appear to be dressed as we wish.

Michelle must have chosen a mission to be part of a dysfunctional family, either to assist the family or to make up for past wrongs or a combination of both. Whatever the facts, even after she passed away she was still trying to protect her family.

David G. also let Michelle possess his body at a later time for Michelle wanted to use David's body to convey to her mother how much she loved her. David G. showed all of the effects of a medium allowing a spirit to use them to communicate to the physical world.

"I actually dropped down onto the floor in a fetal position weeping. My sister in law asked what was the matter. My wife knew. I lay there trying to get a grip and while I was there in that space between physical reality and soul awareness something happened again. Michelle came through. Not verbally, not in words, but lovingly. She asked if she could use my body. There's no way to say how these things happen. There's no real progression of events. It's just all there all at once. Like that void, that place of nothingness where everything is all the time. Just think about it and you're there. Any time any place. It's all one. We're all one."[186]

In Spiritism, David G. would have been trained as to what to expect and how to allow a spirit to temporarily control his body, all the while maintaining the ability to dislodge the spirit when he deemed it necessary. Also, to make sure the situation never spirals out of control, there would be other trained mediums in the room to come to the rescue if the possessed medium felt weak. Again, most probably, Michelle had other souls assisting her in using David G.'s body to convey her message of love.

David G. proved himself most useful. Therefore, given his great talent to help others in need, he started upon a new career.

"I've developed a healing arts practice of my own that became a vocation. Since retiring from my career as a postmaster, and even in the years before retiring, I've turned that vocation into a small business. I practice as a vocation though, not as a business. It's not about money. The money comes all by itself when it's needed. I've never had to worry. Working with people, usually with spiritual and emotional blockages, had been my calling. PTSD (posttraumatic stress disorder) seems to be a common thread among my best clients."[187]

Notice how David G. said, "It's not about money", this is one of the most basic rules of Spiritism, you should not charge money for the gifts that God gives to you; you should freely give to others to help them in their time of need. Knowing this, the spirit world provides for those that contribute their talents freely. David G. is not correct when he says, "The money comes all by itself when it's needed." There is a team of spirits directing events to ensure that his needs and the needs of his family are taken care of.

We are so much closer to the hand of God than any of us could ever believe. We grow up in a society where God is at best distant to most of us. Thankfully, I have found out, late in life, as David G. has, that God's love is so much closer than we realize.

# Section 4 – Where do I go From Here

Now that you understand how we are being guided, we should dive deeper into where is the spirit world and where are the places you want to be and wish to avoid?

After all, once you rid yourself of your physical cocoon, your spirit will find the level where you belong. First you experience a review of your life and are given the opportunity to objectively evaluate your success and failures. Your judgment and attitude is what sends you to your destination. There isn't Saint Peter at the gate determining if you are allowed to enter or be sent down to Hell.

The force that either moves you up, down, or sideways is the Law of Affinity. As discussed earlier, it is the force which associates spirits based on their sympathies. A preponderance of love, charity, spirituality and fraternity propels you higher, where there are many level of Heaven. On the other hand, the dominance of selfishness, materialism and criminal intent sends you to live with those who are just like you. A subtle hint from the spirit world to determine if you really like living with your own kind.

There is also the possibility of hanging around; it's called the "lower zone", or Umbra in Portuguese. It may be compared to the Catholic notion of Purgatory, a temporary place. A location designed to give you the required time to ponder your past life.

The main difference from most religions is that in Spiritism, you determine how long you wish to rub shoulders with your friends, since you always have the choice to turn your deepest feelings around and be a better soul. Unfortunately for many, you have to actually change your thoughts and attitudes, you can't just mouth plentitudes, as countless do in our current world. Of course, include me in that count!

Next, you shall explore how the end game will play out, as we progress from a planet of atonement to one of regeneration. You shall discover the levels above where we are now and beyond.

Truly, after reviewing the future possibilities, you will realize what immature spirits we are. It is humbling to acknowledge that the vast majority of us are mere sprites, learning how to walk and behave.

The vision of the future is important. The spirit world realizes that at this stage of our materialistic culture, where the pull of the latest gadget and the prevailing philosophy is moral relativism, that we could trap ourselves in complacency. Happy to sit watching the mindless entertainment, never making value judgments, except for what clothes a character may be wearing. Whereby one group's blood sacrifices may be compared to Christmas shopping activities of another. Where there are no absolutes there are no boundaries, no guiderails to lead society to the just conclusion and way of life.

While, for many, the phrase "just conclusion and way of life" could harken back to the days hiding your lifestyle from a potential judgmental and abusive society. Spiritism teaches us that we should have the opportunity to learn the basic facts of living together, to love, to be charitable, honorable and inclusive. Love meaning to treat all equally, whether they are in different types of sexual relationships or marriages. The point that is stressed is the holiness of two spirits working together and the family, whatever combination of sexes that may contain. Working as one, helping each other to focus their energy for good is the supreme goal.

At the least, the formation of a society that is just, where one's word is good as gold, where burning envy is absent and all gather to contribute for the betterment of those around them. Yes, an impossible aim given our current status. One only the most delusional fanatic could even consider, but when seen through the prism of thousands of years is not unattainable.

Consider the advances made since the great architecture of Rome was built using a combination of freemen and slave labor. Large parts of the world no longer burn heretics at the stake, no longer are cities captured and all sold into slavery. The world may still secretly admire brute force and naked power, but large sections of the world understands its limitations. People frightened

160

into submission will eventually stop working, thereby causing the slow destruction of the empire built upon fear.

We have gone far and still have far to go, but thanks to the invisible hand of the spirit world, we are traveling in the right direction.

# Chapter 23 - The Other Side of the NDE Judgment Experience

Many people who have had NDE's report that they are judged in their conduct here on earth. Experiences that are replayed to them in the smallest detail. Swedenborg, who wrote eight books about the spirit world, was a witness to many trials. This chapter illustrates a few examples.

## Swedenborg's Heaven and Hell

He writes, in his book, *Heaven and Hell*, about the trials he personally viewed during his time in the spirit world. Swedenborg's main contention is that we retain all, and by all, even the tiniest details, of our entire life while on earth. Hence, these records are used, for and against us, when we pass over. Here is one example of what he wrote:

> "There were people who had deceived others with malicious skill and had stolen from them. Their deceptions and thefts were also recounted one after the other, many of them known to practically no one in the world other than themselves. They even admitted them because they were made plain as day, along with every thought, intention, pleasure, and fear that mingled in their minds at the time."[188]

A truly frightening prospect. Not only the facts of our follies, but even our foolish and misguided thoughts and motivations at the time of the wrong. I am not looking forward to that day! Wait it gets more interesting:

> "There were people who had taken bribes and made money from judicial decisions. They were similarly examined from their own memories, and everything was recounted from their first taking office to the end, The details of amount and value, of the tie, and their state of mind and intention, all consigned to their remembrance together, were brought to view, a hundred or more instances. In some cases, remarkably enough, the very

diaries in which they had recorded those deeds were opened and read to them, page by page."[189]

What a relief, no longer do I have to worry whether the legions of corrupt officials, which I see on news shows every day, will someday receive their just deserts. The ones who managed to pass away in old age, whose last thoughts were that they had successfully used the system, will receive a surprising welcome on the other side. But, I shouldn't think in this manner, for if Spiritism has taught us anything, it is to be charitable and caring for our fellow man. Therefore, I should be grateful for those corrupt souls to have their chance at true self-knowledge and to wish them Godspeed in their next life, where I sincerely wish their attainment for all of their goals for improvement.

We are judged even for our harmful gossip, as illustrated by Swedenborg:

"There was one man who thought of nothing of slandering others. I heard his slanders recounted in sequence as well as his blasphemies, along with the actual words, the people they were about, and the people they were addressed to. All these were presented together as lifelike as could be even though he had very carefully kept them hidden from his victims while he was living in the world."[190]

Therefore, any form of harm to our fellow beings is counted against us.

For the true criminal action, Swedenborg gives us the following harrowing example:

"There was one man who had defrauded a relative of his legacy by some devious pretest. He was exposed and judged in the same way. Remarkably, the letters and documents they exchanged were read aloud to me, and he said not a word was missing. This same man had also secretly killed a neighbor by poison just before his own death, which was disclosed in the following way. A trench seemed to open under his feet, and as it was opened, a man came out as through a tomb and screamed

163

at him, "What have you done to me?" Then everything was disclosed – how the poisoner had talked amicably with him and offered him a drink, what he had thought beforehand, and what happened afterward. Once this was uncovered, the murderer was condemned to hell."[191]

For those who have experienced a trial during an NDE, these descriptions are all too real. For example, Gail, who had a NDE at the age of fourteen, describes her experience, as she remembers it in May, 2014.

"I was aware that I could communicate without speaking and that I could know all that I wanted to know. There was a feeling of peace and calm, unlike anything I've experienced since. Then came a judgment of sorts, where I was judged on the things I had done and the things I would do in my future life. This upset me as I felt it was mean to punish or judge me for things I hadn't done yet. I wasn't judged on big things, more small instances of intent. It was the little things that mattered and not the big things. Then I was told that I had to go back, which didn't make me happy at all as I knew that being alive would hurt."[192]

Heaven and Hell was written in 1749, over 260 years ago. The same process for judging us at our death is still in effect. Spiritism, a gift from the spirit world to us, is here to provide context for people's NDEs. Yes, they are absolutely an experience not of this world, but that isn't the important lesson to take away. It is that there is a spirit world, we are here on earth to learn to become better souls and that all of our actions will be evaluated to determine our grades while in the school of physical life. We are all, without exception, here to travel on our personal journeys to become pure, loving, caring and fraternal spirits.

---

# Chapter 24 – What is Hell – the Dark – the Abyss

After our transformation from our physical bodies to spirit form we exist for a time in the Lower Zone. Since this is the area we resided in while using our dense bodies. After our souls are separated we travel to where the Law of Affinity places us.

The Lower Zone, which shall be discussed in the next chapter is not a nice place to be, one where you are constantly in danger from marauding gangs and living in semi-darkness. A place designed to push you off your previously constructed pedestal that you could live without faith, fraternity and honor.

There is a worse place. And it's not meant to merely change your attitude. Since the people who find themselves drawn down into the abyss don't just have a problem with their approach and outlook, but their entire belief system. Where might makes right and the big stick can whack the heck out of anyone who only possesses a little stick.

It is where the opposite of the Golden Rule, others do unto you as you have done unto others. The spirit realm doesn't call it "Hell", for that would imply a location where errant souls go and stay permanently. The spirit realm calls it the Darkness or the Abyss, sometimes I see it mentioned as a type of purgatory. For spirits are never sent to unalterable situations. God desires all of us to eventually ascend to be a pure spirit. Even though the journey may be torturous and painful. Whenever we find ourselves in real spiritual pain, it is usually because a nice suggestion wasn't absorbed, hence we required a blunter object to attract our attention. The Darkness is a weighty sharp weapon which is specifically designed for those of us who just wouldn't take the hint.

Whereas the Lower Zone starts at the crust of the earth and rises above until it meets the boundary of heaven, the Abyss, hence its name, is beneath the Lower Zone. It descends from the lowest altitude of the Umbral toward the center of the earth.

Andre Luiz, in the book *Liberation*, travels on a mission to the Abyss, he describes the landscape:

"The sun's light looked different.

A grayish haze clouded the entire sky.

Volitation (*definition: ability to move by thought*) was impossible.

The vegetation looked sinister and afflicted. The trees were almost bare and the nearly-dry branches looked like arms lifted in supplication.

Large, foreboding birds that looked sort of like ravens were cawing like little winged monsters eyeing hidden prey.

What was most troubling, however, was not the bleak landscape – it was somewhat similar to others I had experienced – but the piercing appeals coming from the mire. Humanlike groans came in every tone."[193]

The scenes described could be out of any of the movies or books we have seen and read about hell. A desolate landscape, dry and populated with revolting creatures.

Andre also notices gangs, which are wandering around the landscape:

"From time to time, hostile groups of deranged spirit entities passed in front of us, indifferent and incapable of noticing our presence. They were speaking loudly in broken but intelligible Portuguese, their laughter betraying deplorable conditions of ignorance. They were dressed in sinister attire and carried implements for fighting and wounding."[194]

Again, a passage that could be directly lifted from the Tolkien's *Lord of the Rings*. One begins to perceive that our culture interprets the images of purgatory similar because of the

166

inspirations from the spirit world conveys to us the essential truth of the Darkness. From Dante's books, *Inferno* and *Purgatorio*, to Hieronymus Bosch's pictures of hell, we are fed a vision, designed to warn us of what may lie ahead.

Whereas, we in the modern world have discarded such childish notions, because we can't prove beyond a shadow of a doubt the existence of purgatory, we fail to notice the evidence of people's near death experiences. Those minority of people who instead of reuniting with family or feeling part of a universal love and intelligence, are taken to a place where they glimpse what is awaiting them if they remain on their current path.

## Organization of the Abyss

Seeing the strange landscape and the characters which inhabit it, Andre Luiz ask whether this dark region has some sort of organizational structure. The leader of the expedition, Gubio, explains:

"Why wouldn't there be? As in the corporeal sphere, the Higher Powers have endowed this domain with a form of leadership for the time being. This great emporium of regenerative suffering is led by a satrap of unbelievable ruthlessness, who has given himself the pompous title 'Great Judge'. He is assisted by political and religious advisors who are as cold and perverse as he is. A huge aristocracy of implacable spirits controls thousands of idle, morally delinquent, sickly minds."[195]

Hence, there is no commanding devil, but fiefdoms led by individuals who have managed to control small areas of the underworld. Those who were hungry for power and domination in their physical life continued on after death. Climbing the ladder of power in a society designed to punish, albeit temporarily, transgressors whose actions and thoughts drove them to the level on par with their peers. Where the conscience of these poor souls could seek the punishment to eventually rid themselves of their wrongs, only to find themselves in a place worse than they could imagine.

Doesn't this sound, look, and fell like "Hell"? One could ask, why does God allow this? Gubio supplies the answer:

"For the same instructive reasons that God does not exterminate a human nation, when, insane with a thirst for domination, it unleashes cruel and destructive war; instead, he hands it over to the expiation of its crimes and to the misfortune it has brought upon itself, so that it can learn to become part of the eternal order that presides over universal life. Over the course of many centuries, the matter used by those intelligences is worked and restructured, just like in the earthly circles; but if the Lord visits humankind by means of sanctified individuals, he also corrects spirits by means of hardened or beastly ones."[196]

The inmates are in charge. The most hardened criminals who descended here exist to demonstrate that where people who share the same anti-beliefs, meaning anti-love, anti-charity, anti-selflessness and anti-fraternity conjugate, would create a society founded upon only the most base principles. The result of such a culture of hate and selfishness is the perfect location to learn how the world would appear and function if everyone followed the same ideals.

## In one of the Cities of the Darkness

As Andre enters the city, he begins to record the sights as he heads toward the center:

"A short time later, we entered a vast agglomeration of narrow streets lined with sordid and unkempt dwellings.

Loathsome faces eyed us furtively at first, but as we continued on our way, we were scrutinized by hostile and dreadful-looking passersby.

A few miles of public streets filled with heart rendering scenes unrolled before us.

Hundreds of emotionally imbalanced entities, along with

disfigured ones with all sorts of deformities, made up the horrifying picture."[197]

Andre is aghast at the legions of people with obvious imperfections. He inquires how so many have acquired such deformities. His team leader Gubio tells him the sad truth:

"After death, millions of individuals run into dangerous enemies due to fear and self-shame. In the sphere of our actions, words and thoughts, nothing is lost, Andre. The records of our lives works in two distinct phases: outside of us through the effects of our actions regarding our neighbors, situations and affairs as individuals, and within the archives of our conscience, which mathematically records all the results of our good and bad deeds. The spirit acts amid its own creations. Dark imperfections and praiseworthy qualities both envelop it wherever it may be. People on earth, on which we journey, hear arguments alluding to heaven and hell, and they vaguely believe in the spirit life that awaits them after death. Sooner than they might think, they lose the physical body and realize they can no longer hide behind its mask like a turtle in its shell."[198]

We are what we are inside. Every thought, every action we take is recorded by our spirit. Nothing is lost, when we lose our physical shell our true nature exposes itself for all of the universe to see. Most probably, we have all walked the streets of a dark city at one time or another. For we have been primitive souls, ignorant of how to behave and believe. But we have learned through the suffering we have endured that the path of complete selfishness and unbridled passion and greed never pays enough for the price incurred.

## Suffering is the Key for Future Advancement

Why must many suffer so much and for so long? Because not just some of us, but all of us are on the path to perfection. To be perfect means that any anomaly, no matter how infinitesimal, shall be removed. There are always times when we are able to learn by a simple discussion and we take the advice offered to us to heart, but at other periods in our life we remain closed to any suggestions. Secure in our minds that we know better. Suffering scrubs through that layer of obstinacy and cleanses the blemish, that we were unable to remove ourselves.

Allan Kardec's book *Heaven and Hell*, sums up the process, in Chapter VII, Future Punishment According to Spiritism:

"33) In spite of the diversity in the kinds and degrees of punishment that imperfect spirits suffer, the penal code of the future life may be summed up in these three principles:

1. Suffering is inherent to imperfection.

2. Every imperfection as well as every wrong resulting from it brings its own punishment in natural and inevitable consequences. Hence, sickness results from excess, and boredom from laziness, without there having to be some kind of special condemnation for each wrong or individual.

3. Since all people can free themselves from their imperfections by their will, they can annul the ills that result from them and can ensure future happiness.

To each according to his or her deeds, in heaven as well as on earth – such is the law of divine justice."[199]

Therefore, we are now armed with the knowledge that firstly, our deeds are recorded within our spirit memories; secondly, we react to our exploits by the governing process of our conscience. From which, highly evolved spirits are able to read our memories with exact precision; thusly we have nowhere to hide from others the actions we performed. Lastly the divine laws categorize us to the level where we belong.

There is no shortcut, no absolution in our journey of eternity. We have a choice, we can spend eons in denial, fighting the process every step, or we can accept the inevitable and commit our heart and labor to the lesson at hand.

An example of the consequences of taking the easy path is in

170

the book Heaven and Hell. It is a transcript of a session with a spirit who appeared to a medium group without any bidding. He said his name was Benoist and that he had died in 1704. He announced that he was in great agony.

*"1. What were you when alive?*

'A faithless monk.'

*2. Was disbelief your only imperfection?*

'It was enough to lead to others.'

*3. Could you give us some of the details of your life? A sincere confession would be counted in your favor.*

'I was poor and lazy. I entered the order not because I had a call, but in order to have a position. Being intelligent, I found myself one. Being influential, I abused my power. Being corrupt, I corrupted those whom I had the mission of saving. Being cruel, I persecuted those who seemed to disapprove of my excesses. Those at peace were disturbed by me; hunger tortured many of my victims, and their screams were often silenced through violence. Since then, I have been making expiation and have been suffering all the tortures of hell; my victims stir up the fires that devour me. Lechery and insatiable hunger pursue me and thirst burns my parched lips, without a refreshing drop of water ever falling on them. All the elements hound me. Pray for me.'[200]

## The Way Out

Unfortunate Beniost will have to spend his allotted time in his personal torture chamber, but he made the first step in recognizing that his deeds caused the consequences that befell him. Once he starts his introspection, he signals that he is ready to reincarnate to pay his debts. Others who are hopeless causes are also sent to be reborn, but in even more dire circumstances.

Unlike the intricate planning for reincarnation for those spirits who reside in the celestial cites, where they take an active part in

171

planning their life and body down to the last detail, those in the Lower Zones and the Darkness have not earned that privilege.

Andre Luiz, in the book *Workers of the Life Eternal*, learns from a worker in the Lower Zone, how reincarnations are planned for those less fortunate.

"Expiatory reincarnation involving unspeakable suffering follows due to the crushing vibrations of hatred and punishing humiliation. In the fortunate realm in which you reside, there are institutions that take into account suggestions involving a spirit's personal choice. Free will – that guarantor of natural credit – may request changes and present fair demands, but here the conditions are different … Uncivilized, indebted souls cannot be satisfied with regards to their preferences concerning their own future due to the deliberate ignorance in which they have taken pleasure for who knows how long. And in accordance with those who guide them from the upper realms, they are compelled to accept the itineraries set by the authorities responsible for their individual cases."[201]

All are allowed an end to their painful warning and are given another chance to return to the physical world where a series of events shall again test their mettle. Can they use their free-will to make the choices which illustrate they have learned the divine lessons presented to them, or will they once more prove to be unworthy to ascend to an advanced level?

Only time will tell, after all there is an eternity waiting for them in which they can either waste life after life in obstinate denial or begin to improve, step by step, up the ladder that is in front of everyone of us. Steps to perfection and a happy productive life in the service of others is the light at the end of the tunnel.

# Chapter 25 – What is the Lower Zone – not Hell and not Heaven

"The Lower Zone", this is where we enter our physical bodies and where we leave them. We have all been there for longer periods, between lifetimes at one epoch or another. It's a place where not horrible and not spiritual people go to after they leave their body. It's meant to be a temporary location, a way station, for those who haven't yet made up their minds to follow the ways of love, charity, fraternity, and honesty. When one finally realizes the benefits of the golden rule, and the overriding love of God, then the door is unlocked and you are assisted out and up to a higher level. A celestial city.

What exactly is the Lower Zone like? Andre Luiz, who woke up there after his death on the operating room table describes one small part of it:

"Actually, I felt like a prisoner trapped behind dark bars of horror. With my hair on end, my heart pounding, and scared stiff, I often cried out like a madman. I begged for mercy and clamored against the painful despondency that had taken hold of my spirit. But when the loud cries didn't fall on an implacable silence, they were answered by lamenting voices even more pitiful than my own. At other times, sinister laughter rent the prevailing silence. I thought that some unknown companion out there was a prisoner of insanity. Diabolical forms, ghastly faces, animal-like countenances appeared from time to time, increasing my panic."[202]

Doesn't seem like a great place does it? The Lower Zone is comprised of many areas. Not just a strange dark dimension that exists parallel to our own, but also right here, on the surface of the earth.

In the book, *Memoirs of a Suicide*, by Yvonne A. Pereira, the main protagonist of the book, Camilo Castelo Branco, who committed suicide when he was going blind because of syphilis, describes what it was like awaking in the graveyard where he was buried.

"Sobbing uncontrollably, I bent over the grave that held my wretched remains. Contorting myself in terrifying convulsions of pain and rage, wallowing in a crisis of diabolical fury, I understood that I had committed suicide, that I was in the grave, but that, nevertheless, I continued to live and suffer even more, so much more than before, superlatively, abysmally so much more than before my cowardly and thoughtless act!"[203]

Hence, Camilo, while his body, six feet underground, was deteriorating, felt he was alive, with all of the loneliness, pain and suffering it entails. Walking on the face of the earth, while incarnate visitors to familial graves passed through him, oblivious to his sufferings.

Camilo then left the cemetery, trying to ascertain what was this world that he had died into?

"I continued to roam around aimlessly, feeling my way along the streets, unacknowledged by friends and admirers, a poor blind man humiliated in the afterlife thanks to the dishonor of having committed suicide; a beggar in the spirit world, famished in the darkness; a tortured, wandering ghost without a home, without shelter in the immense and infinite world of spirits; exposed to deplorable dangers; hounded by malefic entities, criminals of the spirit world, who love to use hateful traps to capture individuals going through tormenting situations like mine in order to enslave then and increase the obsessing hordes that destroy earth's societies and ruin men and women, submitting them to the vilest temptations with their deadly influence."[204]

The Lower Zone is all around us, teeming with life, not of the benevolent kind. The type of life that we discarded as childish fears long ago. That our rational minds refused to consider, since we could neither touch nor see it. For even if there are multiple instances of unexplainable phenomena, unless we have positive proof, or see it on television or the internet, we are labeled fools to believe its existence.

Exists it does and it is there for a purpose. While we must go through trials in our physical life, in order to learn the valuable lessons assigned to us, once we end our studies, does everyone pass? No matter how pitiful our performance was? We aren't in our local kindergarten class where each participant gets a ribbon. God is love, and love can be tough love, the love that holds us to a high standard. A raised bar that ensures only those who meet the minimum criteria are allowed to enter.

Does God decide for each of us what our grades were and where we go onto next? No, it is accomplished much more efficiently, the Law of Affinity, filters us out rather nicely. The law which combines like with like, reprobate with reprobate, selfishness with selfishness, dividing us by a thousand little gates into the group to where we precisely belong. If we have balanced our life with spirituality and materialism, so we are not bound by earthly objects we may rise above the Lower Zone. On the other hand, if we live a life of lusting after the newest gadget, the biggest house, stepping on others on our way to prosperity, then we get to stay with souls just like us. No wonder there are gangs of criminal spirits waiting for their next victim amongst the dead. For the place is full of those who gleefully took advantage of others whenever possible.

## The Lower Zone or Umbral

The Brazilian Spiritist call the Lower Zone, the Umbral. A much better name, if a friend asked you, "Have you been to the Lower Zone?" wouldn't you rather reply, "Me? No, but I have visited the Umbral for a time." Sounds more exotic, with a splash of Italian architecture thrown in, hinting that the food must be prepared relatively well there.

In the book, *Nosso Lar*, psychographed by Chico Xavier and inspired by Andre Luiz; Andre, after being rescued from the Umbral by the kind spirits of the heavenly city, Nosso Lar, asks why must there be a place like the Lower Zone. He receives an answer from his friend Lisias:

175

"Imagine that when we reincarnate, each of us is wearing a dirty garment that must be washed in the waters of human life. This dirty garment is our casual body, woven by our own hands during our past lives. As we share in the blessings of a new earthly opportunity once more, we usually forget our essential purpose, and instead of purifying ourselves through the effort of the cleansing process, we become even more soiled by going deeper into debt and thus imprisoning ourselves in genuine slavery. Now if we return to the world seeking a way to rid ourselves of our impurities because they are out of harmony with a higher plane, how can we expect to enter the sphere of light in an even worse state than before? Therefore, the Umbral is a region intended for the flushing away of negative mental residues. It is a sort of purgatorial zone, where one gradually burns off the refuse of the bulk of illusions acquired after having degraded the sublime opportunity of an earthly life."[205]

Lisias explains to Andre, that the Umbral begins at the crust of the earth and continues higher until it reaches the boundaries of the celestial cities. A large area that contains all those who couldn't successfully complete their mission, souls that retained their passions for material goods, hatred of their enemies, and a host of other obsessions that we are all better without.

Lisias emphasizes this point by describing the criticality of the zone.

"The Umbral is a region of profound importance for those still on earth, for it embodies everything that is useless to the more highly evolved life. Consider how wisely Divine Providence has acted in allowing the creation of such a zone around the planet. There are legions of irresolute and ignorant souls, who are not wicked enough to be relegated to the colonies of the most dolorous expiation, nor are they sufficiently virtuous to be admitted to the higher planes. They represent the ranks of the inhabitants in the Umbral, and they are close companions of incarnate human beings, separated from them only by vibratory laws."[206]

The phrase, "embodies everything that is useless", is the key to all. Useless are material goods. Useless are the passions we retain, the revenge we are plotting even up to our untimely death. Useless is our quest for a lavish lifestyle that compromised our ideals and forced us to ignore our conscience in order to gain a moment of wealth. Wealth, that is no longer with us while we reside in the Umbral.

As if our life on earth isn't difficult enough for us, there is another hurdle awaiting those who fail to absorb the message that we must improve our spiritual life while surviving the planned events that we have signed up for.

## Organization of the Lower Zone

The Umbral is composed of unfortunate souls, who lacked the required faith to believe in life after death, people who were aimless in their physical existence, financial and petty criminals. When Andre was in the Umbral, he did notice groups of spirits, he asks how the Lower Zone is organized:

"Organization is an attribute of organized spirits. What do you expect? The lower zone to which we are referring is like a home where there is no food: Everyone whines and no one is reasonable. The absent-minded traveler misses the train; the farmer who does not sow cannot reap. However, there is only one thing I can say for sure: Even in the darkness and anguish of the Umbral, divine watch-care is never lacking. Each spirit remains there just as long as is absolutely necessary, and that is why the Lord has permitted the establishment of many colonies like this one, devoted to useful work and spiritual aid."[207]

Hence, there is no over-all structure commanding the Lower Zone. It is a collection of different geographical areas with an everlasting flow of souls in and out of the regions. As people die, those who do not have the capacity to rise above, remain in the Umbral, while those who have served enough time to readjust their thinking and discover the possibilities of a better life, and find a place in a spiritual colony to begin their climb to spiritual health.

This is not to say, that there are not gangs of individual spirits who try and carve out their territories. For why should the Umbral be any different than on earth? The people who strived to take advantage of others find their kinsmen and quickly look to replicate their past deeds.

Sometimes they actively war to gain their terrain. In the book, *Action and Reaction*, Andre Luiz is visiting a small colony, more like a fort, located deep in the Umbral. Its purpose is to help those who desire to escape their time in that desolate region. The center's name is "Mansao Paz", which translates into "Mansion of Peace".

Andre describes the weapons that defend the small colony, as a series of metallic poles which are charged to repel any attacks. Andre witnesses one such attack and asks:

"Are we being attacked by an army?" I asked, intrigued.

"Yes, we are," Druso confirmed calmly. "These attacks are common, however. Our unfortunate brothers are trying to force us to move our building and render us powerless so that they can take over the region."[208]

The attackers are equipped with canons that discharge harmful vibrations that would cause terror and madness, if it wasn't for the defenses of the fort. Which illustrates that indeed, some type of organized criminal groupings are present. Wherever, there is control by criminals, there exist the need for them to enslave the weak and feeble. There are always legions of henchmen ready to do their bidding in the hopes of rising to the top one day.

The presence of cannons, which are capable of spreading fear, indicates a sophisticated supply chain. There must be collectives within the Lower Zone which can manufacture weapons and probably other goods.

All of this is occurring right at our doorstep. As we walk, as we drive, as we work, we are swimming in the same space as the Lower Zone. Millions of forlorn and discarded creatures emanating negative thoughts and energy. We are living in an atmosphere charged with rays designed to bring us down, to their level. No wonder we must struggle daily with keeping our heads uplifted.

All of this is by design. We live on a planet of atonement, where we must pay for our past wrongs. We must expiate our mistakes. While doing so, we live in an atmosphere where at any time we can breathe in adverse forces to kick us off the right path. In order to succeed in our trials, we must demonstrate pure dedication, in our hearts and minds, to living a life deserving our entrance to a celestial city.

# Chapter 26 - What is Heaven Like

We now know what to avoid. Life in the Lower Zone or the Darkness is not pleasant. It's not meant to be. The environments below the celestial cities serve to spur us toward the correct decisions. Choices which enable us to enter where we all desire.

Everyone wants to know what Heaven is like. Spiritism was brought to us so you would know. The answers are in Allan Kardec's *The Spirits Book* and in books psychographed by Francisco C. Xavier. This chapter will explain Heaven and its different levels and what spirits do there. Hint: It's not eternal leisure.

The quest to begin the search for what is heaven like, starts with Allan Kardec's *The Spirits Book*. Allan Kardec organized a series of questions designed to discern the exact nature and wishes of the spirits. He did not accept information from just one medium, but verified the response to a question from multiple mediums throughout Europe.[209] Some well-known people have been Spiritist, such as Thomas Edison and Sir Arthur Conan Doyle. The questions and answers about Heaven is way in the back of the book. The idea of heaven is not a major preoccupation of the Spirits. They take it matter-of-fact, as a place where they still work and learn and hope to improve themselves. Although, even the lowest rung of heaven is much superior to our planet. And yes, there are many levels, how many is not known to us. Therefore, we will concentrate on just the first level, where if I am lucky, I will get to see. Let's start at that question at the end of the book:

*1016. In what sense is the word heaven to be understood?*

"Do you suppose it to be a place like the Elysian Fields of the ancients, where all good spirits are crowded together pell-mell, with no other care than that of enjoying, throughout eternity, a passive felicity? No; it is universal space; it is the planets, the stars, and all the worlds of high degree, in which spirits are in the enjoyment of all their faculties, without having the tribulations of material life, or the sufferings inherent in the state of inferiority."[210]

Not the Elysian Fields, not the place where you leisurely waste away your days for infinity. For a description of one of the higher levels of heaven, we can go to the book, *Renunciation*, written by the spirit Emmanuel and psychographed by Francisco C. Xavier in Brazil in 1944, it is a story set in the 17th century earth, but in the beginning pages the high level spirit Alcyone is planning on returning to earth to help her love. The passage describes a high level heaven:

"Soon thereafter, she was in a wonderful sphere, indescribable in its magnificence and grandeur. The splendorous sight of it exceeded anything that could ever characterize beauty in the human sense. The sacred vision of its entirety was far beyond the famous city of the saints as idealized by the thinkers of Christianity. Three blazing suns poured oceans of magnificent light onto the ermine ground in unique changes of color, like celestial lamps lighted for the paradisiacal feast of immortal spirits. Exquisite building, surrounded with indescribable flowers, took the form of castles carved with golden filigree, radiating multi-color effects. Winged beings came and went in pursuits of sanctified purposes, in an endeavor of a superior nature, inaccessible to the understanding of earthlings.

Dominated by inexpressible thoughts, Alcyone entered a temple of majestic proportions. High above the radiant sanctuary rose a translucent tower made of a solid, transparent substance similar to crystal. Harmonious melodies pointed forth from within it.

The majestic shrine was a colossal hive of work and prayer."[211]

Doesn't this sound marvelous? Well, don't get too excited, you probably aren't going there, I know I'm not. This is a description of a heaven for high and purified spirits. For the overwhelming majority of us, we will need to set our sights lower. This is not to say that someday many of us won't attain such an exalted level.

# A Heaven above Earth

Another book psychographed by Francisco C. Xavier, is *Nossa Lar*, which means our home. The book was dictated by the spirit Andre Luiz, who was a doctor in Rio de Janeiro, probably in the early 1900's. This was his first book, written in 1944, Andre Luiz dictated more books to Xavier, one of his books *And Life Goes On*, was written in 1968. The story of Nossa Lar is the journey of Andre from his death to his arrival at the celestial city of Nossa Lar. He describes his first impression upon being outside of the shelter he was taken to during his recovery:

> "The spectacle of the streets impressed me. Wide avenues bordered with trees. Pure air – an atmosphere of profound spiritual tranquility. However, there was no sign of inactivity or idleness, for the city streets were crowded. Countless individuals were coming and going. Some seemed to be thinking of far-off places, but others looked at me warmly."[212]

In all descriptions we have read so far, there exists a sense of organization. Structures representing our organizations, such as well-planned roads, houses, people going about in a logical manner. Or should I say, that we here on earth are a poor reflection of heaven, we try to organize as our spirit guided intuition tells us, but our efforts fall short of perfection.

The first level of heaven actually has a system of governance. And why shouldn't it, in heaven would we all be a chaotic mixture of souls with no purpose? The civil structure is described as follows:

> "During our collective prayers, haven't you seen our spirit Governor, surrounded by his seventy-two assistants? Well they are the Ministers of Nossa Lar. The colony's purpose is essentially labor and production, and is divided into six Ministries, each under the direction of twelve Ministers. There are the Ministries of Regeneration, Assistance, Communication, Elucidation, Elevation and Divine Union. The first four connect us with the terrestrial spheres, the remaining two link us with the higher planes; thus, our spirit city is a

transition zone. The Ministry of Regeneration carries out the most ordinary services, whereas the most sublime ones belong to the Ministry of Divine Union."[213]

You may ask, why the name Nossa Lar, am I going to a place where I must speak Portuguese? No, for the cities that represent the first level of heaven are located above numerous geographical areas on earth. If you live in London, for instance, you would probably rise up to a celestial city somewhere above England. Nossa Lar wasn't founded until the sixteen century, after the first Portuguese settlers arrived in the Rio de Janeiro area. Once there, they found the spirits of the native inhabitants and worked building the city as it stands today.[214]

Therefore, when we lose our physical bodies, we lose the matter clothing us on earth, but we still have the form of our human existence. Our thoughts create our form in the manner that we think of ourselves, which is usually in our twenties and thirties in heaven. We appear to have a physical form, but made of less dense material. Material that we on earth have no ability to perceive.

Heaven is a beautiful place to live, as Andre Luiz describes the countryside:

"The scenery in front of me was of sublime beauty. The forest was in full bloom and the fresh air was embalmed with an intoxication fragrance. It was all an extraordinary gift of color and mellow light. A large river wound its way leisurely between luxuriant grassy banks sprinkled with blue flowers. The water ran by so peacefully, so crystalline that it seemed tinted in sky blue, mirroring the color of the firmament. Wide pathways cut through the green landscape. Leafy trees were planted at regular intervals along them, offering friendly shade like pleasant shelters in the light of the comforting sun. Fancifully-shaped benches invited one to rest."[215]

The description of the vividness of the colors and the natural beauty parallels other descriptions of heaven by people who have had near death experiences.

## Occupations in Heaven

So, what do people do in this heaven? Prepare yourself for bad news, it's not all leisure and fun all of the time. But think carefully, which of us could stand that? Don't we wish to be useful beings, contributing to a cause greater than our own? Led by people who have the position based entirely on merit, with centuries of experience behind them. A description of the types of work is given to Andre Luiz:

"We are no longer on the sphere of the globe, where discarnate spirits are compulsorily promoted to ghost status. No, we live in an environment of hard work. The jobs in the Ministry of Assistance are laborious and complex; the duties in the Ministry of Regeneration require strenuous effort; those in Communication demand a high standard of individual responsibility; in Elucidation, they require a great capacity for work and profound intellectual values; those in the Ministry of Elevation require self-denial and spiritual enlightenment; lastly, the activities in the Ministry of Divine Union require right wisdom and the application of sincere universal love. The Government Center, in its turn, is the busy seat of all the administrative activities, and numerous services are under its direct control, such as nutrition, electric energy, traffic and transportation, among others. Actually, the law of rest is strictly observed here, so that certain workers do not become overburdened that others. But the law of labor is also strictly adhered to. As for rest and relaxation, the only exception is the Governor himself, who never uses what he is entitled to in this respect." [216]

There is a wide range of occupations in heaven, something for everyone who wishes to contribute. Although, with my resume, I will be lucky to get a job painting the white lines in the center of the roads.

What about those who don't wish to work? What happens to them? Do they starve? Andre Luiz describes a woman who is requesting permission to return to earth, in spirit form, to look after her family. She goes to the Minister of Assistance, Clarencio, to make her request:

"I would like to be granted the means of watching over my children myself in the physical sphere!" replied the afflicted mother.

"I am sorry, my friend," said the loving benefactor, "but only in the spirit of humility and service are we able to watch over someone. What would you say about an earthly father who wanted to provide for his children, but then remained idle in the comfort of his home? The Father has created labor and cooperation as laws that no one may break without causing damage to himself. What does your conscience have to say on the matter? How many hour-bonuses can you present for your request?"

The woman answered hesitantly; "Three hundred and four."

"It's a pity," continued Clarencio, smiling, "that you have lived here for over six years but have given the colony only three hundred and four hours of work. However, as soon as you recovered from the struggles you had suffered in the lower regions, I offered you a praiseworthy job on the Vigilance Team of the Ministry of Communication..."

"But that was intolerable work," she interrupted, "a constant struggle with malevolent entities! Of course I couldn't adapt to it."[217]

Let's do the calculation, she has worked three hundred and four hours over a six year period. Hence, she has worked a little less than eight forty hour weeks. Not bad, to be clothed and fed, over six years for only working a total of two months. In Nossa Lar, everyone receives their required provisions and clothing, but for extras, such as enjoying entertainment centers, or taking in lectures at different schools, one needs the hour-bonus credit. All receive, no matter what level of work, the same amount per hour. There are exceptions for sacrificial services where the hour-bonus is doubled or tripled.[218]

Her dialogue with the Minister continued through a whole litany of jobs the woman attempted but abandoned after a few furtive days of effort. One can determine that she has no urge to perform any meaningful service. Therefore, most probably she will be reincarnated into a position where she will learn the value of hard work. After all, while God has infinite love, God does not allow infinite leisure, for how else will we be incented to improve ourselves and others.

### Families in Heaven

As in many NDE's and movies, when people go to heaven, they reunite with family members. Often families live in the same house, just as it was on earth. Some members leave for a reincarnation experience, with their house and family members waiting for them on their return. Given the variety of life on earth, and the fact of multiple lives, there are some unusual circumstances which occur. Andre Luiz is invited into the home of his friend Tobias, and he meets Hilda and Luciana. Tobias tells him about his family situation:

> "I believe I should tell you about my two wives; what do you think?"
>
> "Oh, well, yes," I murmured, extremely confused. "You mean that both Hilda and Luciana shared your earth experience?"
>
> "That's right," he answered calmly.
>
> Hilda cut in and said: "Please, excuse our Tobias, brother Andre. He is always eager to talk about the past whenever we meet with someone newly arrived from earth."
>
> "Shouldn't it be a cause for joy," added Tobias with good humor, "to have defeated the monster of jealousy, and to have gained at least a small degree of fraternity?"[219]

Just as on earth there are a multitude of families and relationships. The one important difference is that families in heaven are together based on affinity, their love and longing to be

186

with one another, binds them. Those who have no wish to be part of a particular family, will find their own group, where shared principles and interests create a strong loving bond.

Given all of the above, isn't heaven a bit familiar to you, similar to earth, only better? Without the hate, envy, selfishness or crime of any sort. A place where your own effort is rewarded, not leveraged by someone for personal gain. Heaven, at least the first level, is a stepping stone to an even more elevated existence, a place where through our desire to learn, not only intellectually, but also the joy of fraternity and unconditional love will result in your ascendance into a higher plane. A place where once you arrive, I would appreciate it, if you could tell me about it.

# Chapter 27 - What am I afraid of the most about the Spirit World? – Bureaucracy!

Knowing that heaven is a similar, but a more perfect version of our society on earth, does worry me. Organizations exists in the spirit realm. Organizations need rules, procedures and processes. All contribute to bureaucracy and red-tape.

My biggest fear of dying isn't hell or being locked into some territory of my own mind, but having to live for eternity in a society where incompetent bureaucrats determine our actions and imprison us in their idiotic rules. Where I would have to work with souls who do not merit my respect. Is this fear real or false?

As Spiritist, we realize that when we leave our corporeal bodies, we enter the spirit world, where we are expected to begin to toil, to perform work for the good of the society. Of this, I have no problem, for I completely agree with the comments by the spirits in the book *Heaven and Hell*, where in explaining what is heaven? We are told, "The bliss of the blessed spirits does not consist in contemplative idleness, which, as we have stated many times, would be eternal and fastidious uselessness. On the contrary, spirit life at all degrees involves constant activity, but an activity without weariness." [220]

Constant activity is my normal state, I live to learn, to explore, to do something useful for myself and others. What abhors me are the obstacles put in place by mindless functionaries, people who have nothing better to do than to exercise their petty powers to prove themselves to be bigger than they actually are. The do-gooders who create rules upon rules, a mountain of laws, each one present just to tell me what to do in my daily life, as if I was incapable of any initiative of my own.

## Why I am Worried?

Once you start reading the various books, specifically the

books by Andre Luiz, one detects the constant presence of rules and authority. The existence of a command structure of processes, procedures, and laws which are implied in many passages. Ranging from the small, such as, Andre Luiz who wishes to attend a lecture, writes, "Since I was aware that I needed permission to attend, I asked Tobias about it."[221] Therefore, Andre Luiz couldn't just show up, or buy a ticket, he needed to ask permission. Why should he ask permission? Why couldn't he just go, if that is what he wants? Why? Why must I be controlled even in death? Well, Tobias supplies a sensible answer:

> "These lectures" he said, "are only attended by truly interested spirits. Our instructors can't afford to waste their time. Thus, you will be allowed to attend along with hundreds of other listeners from among the workers and patients of the Ministries of Regeneration and Assistance."

> With an encouraging gesture, he concluded:

> "I hope you really enjoy it."[222]

Ok, well that made sense. Even spirits have the right to not waste their time. There is another passage from the book, *Memoirs of a Suicide*, where a recent suicide, Jeronimo, demanded to see the head physician. Jeronimo was ready for battle:

> "Jeronimo – who thought he would meet with the haughtiness of earthly bureaucrats, stagnated in the foolish boasting they enjoy so much and to which he accustomed – was amazed to perceive in those scrutinizing eyes the humility of a tear oscillating near the surface."[223]

The head physician, Teocrito, was an unexpected find for Jeronimo. A humble and caring leader. Teocrito brings Jeronimo into his office and gently explains:

> "My friend! My brother Jeronimo!" Teocrito began. "Before answering your request, I must first clarify that I am not at all a Prince, as you have supposed, nor do I carry any such titles. I am simply a spirit that used to be a man! Someone who has

lived, suffered and struggled throughout many existences on the earth, learning along the way a few things related to the planet. A servant of Jesus of Nazareth – that is what I am happy to be, albeit very modest, lacking any merits and still very deficient. A plain worker, who, around those who suffer, is taking his first steps in the cultivation of the Divine Master's services of Mary of Nazareth, his august Mother!"[224]

It would be hard to hold any type of prolonged anger at such a bureaucrat. Not to mention, a bit difficult to maintain any higher moral authority. Therefore, after what I have read in the encounters with decision makers in the Spirit world, they seem to be in their positions because they have earned them. What is more astounding, is they genuinely desire to do the right thing.

How many of us have worked in an organization with people like this? I know, that on rare occasions, where I have had the privilege to labor alongside a group of competent, caring and involved people, where we have a leader that treats of all us fairly and we actually admire that person. Unfortunately, this situation never lasts long. Why? Because, some power hungry, incompetent, but politically astute, idiot maneuvers our bright shining leader into an unfair political fight and takes over. I have seen this occur too frequently.

What about the big pronouncements, such as a grand policy decision that could affect many of us in one of the heavenly cities? How are these handled? There is an example of one in the book, *Nossa Lar*. In Nossa Lar, which is an astral city above Rio de Janeiro, which is where the wonderful spirit author Andre Luiz lives, the spirits there do not require meals as we do on earth, they are able to survive perfectly on a smaller portion of nutrients, such as water and sunlight. Although, some spirits still wanted to eat as they did before, fresh from their memories on earth. When Andre first came to the colony Nossa Lar, he learned of the struggle to change the habits of the people there:

"After twenty-one years of persevering effort by the Government Center, the Ministry of Elevation gave in and cut it supplies down to what was strictly necessary. The Ministry of Elucidation, however took much longer to make a commitment due to the great numbers of spirits working there, who were dedicated to the mathematical sciences. They were the most obstinate adversaries. Since there were used to the ingestion of protein and carbohydrates, which they deemed indispensable to the physical body, they wouldn't give in to the new concept applied here. They sent the Governor weekly lengthy observations and warnings full of analyses and numerical data, and they became quite indiscrete at times. The old Governor never acted alone, however. He enlisted the assistance of noble mentors who guide us via the Ministry of Divine Union, and never dismissed even the smallest report without have examined it in detail."[225]

Twenty-one years to get people to gradually change their habits, not exactly an iron-fisted dictatorship. In fact, subtle changes made their way back into the old habits, as told to Andre Luiz:

"Since then, there has been a greater supply of nutritive substances that remind us of earth – but only in the Ministries of Regeneration and Assistance, where there is always a great number in need of such substances."[226]

While, heaven is not a democracy, where people could vote themselves all sorts of destructive devices to amuse the populace, it is a meritocracy, in the purest sense. A true Plato's republic, where the wise, and they actually are wise, not born or maneuvered into their positions, rule.

## Conclusion

What is my conclusion? Yes, there is a bureaucracy in heaven, is it perfect? Probably not. Is it staffed with power hungry political hacks? No. The evidence suggests the people in position of responsibility should be there.

Once again, the Law of Affinity (where like attracts like) rules. Good spirits, who are dedicated to the long toil of excellence have

191

gathered together to guide over us. It's hard to fight loving and caring competent people, it's not a pleasant fight and therefore better to mimic their humbleness and learn from those wiser than you. Be patient in the knowledge that everyone is actively striving for the same object, to assist all of us to attain perfection one day.

# Chapter 28 - The Apocalypse

I have stated before that we are in a time of transformation. Where our planet will become a regenerative world. Hence, this change, this modifying of the human race, our culture, and our technology is the Apocalypse.

For Christians the Apocalypse is a series of calamitous events. Disasters that would affect the entire planet. But according to Spiritism, the earth will change, yes, disasters will occur, but overall our planet will convert gradually. Here we shall learn how the process will work and what we are heading toward.

To understand the coming changes to our world, one must first know where is our planet on the evolutionary scale. Where has it come from and where is it going. For we are all passengers and wouldn't it be nice to identify our destination?

## Levels of Planets

In the book, *The Gospel According to Spiritism*, by Allan Kardec, in Chapter 3, there is an explanation of the different worlds that spirits will inhabit during their long trek toward purification. I will present just a quick summary here, for we shall dive deeper into the future of our entire planet in a later chapter.

1. Primitive World - Intended for the first incarnations of the human soul. The beings that inhabit them are, to a certain extent, rudimentary. They have the human form but are devoid of any beauty. Their instincts are not tempered by any sentiment of refinement or benevolence, or by any notions of right or wrong. Brute force is the only law. With no industry or inventions, they spend life in conquest of food. The earth was once a primitive world.

2. World of Trial and Expiation - You are living on this world. There is more evil present than good. Now you know why life is not easy, because it is not supposed to be while you are reincarnated on the planet Earth.

3. Regenerative World - Where souls still have something to expiate (pay off the debt of a past sin) and may absorb new strength by resting from the fatigue of struggle. There is still evil, but much reduced, the good outweighs the evil, consequently there is no motive for hatred or discord.

4. Happy Worlds - Where good outweighs evil. On Happy Worlds, we still retain our human form, although the senses are more acute.

5. Heavenly or Divine Worlds - Where good reigns completely, all inhabitants are purified spirits. There is no evil.

## The New Testament Apocalypse

Given that the earth is a planet of expiation or atonement, the spirit realm is actively involved in moving us to a better spiritual plane. The spirit Emmanuel, who was the spirit guide for Francisco C. Xavier, and who inspired many books psychographed by Francisco, wrote in his book, *On the Way to the Light*, about the reasons for the spirit world to send the revelations to John:

"A few years before the end of the first century after the coming of the new doctrine, the powers of the spirit world made an analysis of the dreadful situation of the world in view of the future.

The Divine Master called to the higher spheres the spirit John, who was still being held prisoner by the bonds of the earth, and the astonished, afflicted Apostle read the symbolic language of the invisible world.

The Lord told him to deliver his knowledge to the planet as a warning to all the nations and peoples of the earth, and the old Apostle of Patmos transmitted the extraordinary warnings of the Apocalypse to his disciples.

All of the events posterior to John's life are foreseen therein. Certainly, the Apostle's description frequently enters the obscurest terrain. One can plainly see that his human language could not faithfully replicate the divine expression of his visions of remarkable interest for the history of mankind: the wars, the ideological struggles of western civilization are all foreseen in minute detail. And its most dreadful image, which even today is still offered to the eyes of the modern world, is that of the deviant Church of Rome, symbolized as the beast clothed in purple and drunk on the blood of the saints."[227]

Let's look at a summary of part of the New Testament Apocalypse, Chapter 13, and then analyze it through the eyes of the spirit Emmanuel:

"Chapter 13: A Beast comes out of the sea. It has ten horns, seven heads containing diadems and blasphemous names. Like a leopard, but paws like a bear and mouth like a lion. It is given power, throne and authority by the Dragon. One head was mortally wounded and healed. In wonderment, the whole world followed after the Beast. People worshiped Beast and Dragon. Their authority to last only forty two months. Granted authority over all people, nation and race. Worshiped by all those who do not have their names in book of life.

*Let him who has* ears *heed these words: If one is destined for captivity, into captivity he goes! If one is destined to be slain by the sword, by the sword he will be slain! Such is the faithful endurance that distinguishes God's holy people.* A Second Beast comes up out of the Earth. It used the authority of the first Beast *to promote its interests by making the world worship the first beast whose mortal wound had been healed.* Performs great miracles, leads astray Earth's inhabitants by telling them to make an idol of first Beast. Life is given to the image of the Beast, and the power of speech and the ability to put to death anyone who refuses to worship it. Forces all men, rich and poor to accept a stamped image on right hand or forehead. No one allowed *to buy or sell anything unless first marked with the name of the beast or the number that stood for its name. A certain wisdom is needed here; with a little ingenuity anyone can calculate the number of the beast, for it is a number that stands for a certain man. The man's number is six hundred sixty-six.*"[228]

First we are told the authority of the beast will last forty-two months, according to Emmanuel, the correct interpretation is:

"The Apocalypse states that the beast would stay great and blasphemous for 42 months, adding that his number would be 666 (Rev. 18:5,18). By examining the importance of symbols at that time and following a certain course of interpretation, we can take each month as being 30 years instead of 30 days; hence, there is a period of 1,260 years, which is precisely the period 610-1870 of our era, when the Papacy was consolidated from the time of its appearance with the emperor Phocus in 607 to the decree of papal infallibility by Pius IX in 1870, which marked the decadence and absence of Vatican' authority in light of humankind's scientific, philosophic and religious evolution."[229]

Therefore the beast is the Catholic Church, which became corrupted over time, forgetting that it is the church who is to serve, not the populace to serve the church. Emmanuel tells us of many occasions when the spirit world attempted to bring the church back to its beginnings. One such effort is when one of Jesus' apostles reincarnated as Saint Francis of Assisi. Saint Francis tried to demonstrate, by example, that the church was meant to go out and help people, not to just collect money or to stay locked up in monasteries.

What about the famous number 666? If the Catholic Church was the beast, what does the number 666 signify? Again, Emmanuel has the answer:

"As for the number 666, without referring to the interpretations using Greek numerals, but rather using the Roman numerals because they were the most widespread and well-known, we must keep in mind that the Supreme Pontiff of the Roman Church uses the titles "VICARIVS GENERALIS DEI IN TERRIS", "VICARIVS FILII DEI" and "DVX CLERI", which mean, respectively, "God's Chief Vicar on Earth", "Vicar of the Son of God" and "Captain of the Clergy." All one needs is a little game of patience, adding up the Roman numerals found in each papal title, and one will find the same results of 666 in each one of them."[230]

Hence, the beast were the Popes who contributed to the churches journey from simple gathering places, where people congregated to discuss the teaching of Jesus and to assist those in need, to the builder of wealth for the religious class at the top, by siphoning the hard-earned money of millions of peasants. To the present day Catholic Church's benefit, they have reformed themselves into a more benevolent organization, performing many good services for their flock.

## The Spiritist Apocalypse

So, how will the Apocalypse, according to Spiritism, occur? The end will come, but it will come for those low spirits who did not care to learn from their successive lives on this planet. As more spirits understand what it means to be selfless, charitable, and honorable in all circumstances, thereby shedding the constant striving for material goods, they will remain within the earth's sphere, whether in spiritual or physical form. The good spirits will vie for the honor of assisting the transformation of the planet.

The last question of the one thousand and nineteen questions in *The Spirits Book*, tells us exactly how the Apocalypse rolls out:

*1019. Will the reign of goodness ever be established upon the earth?*

"Goodness will reign upon the earth, when, among the spirits who come to dwell in it, the good shall be more numerous than the bad; for they will then bring in the reign of love and justice, which are the source of good and happiness."[231]

Hence, as more people are truly good, the weight of the culture will influence others to follow their example. Those living will have some time to improve themselves, to turn away from the pursuit of coinage by any means. Others will not be so lucky; The Spirits Book tells us their fate:

"The spirits of the wicked people who are mowed down each day by death, and of all who endeavor to arrest the onward movement, will be excluded from the earth, and compelled to incarnate themselves elsewhere; for they would be out of place among those nobler races of human beings, whose felicity would be impaired by their presence among them. They will be sent into never worlds, less advanced than the earth, and will then fulfill hard and laborious missions, which will furnish them with the means of advancing, while contributing also to the advancement of their brethren of those younger worlds, less advanced than themselves."[232]

The people who continue to behave badly will have a surprise waiting for them when they expire. Waking up in the spirit world and then expecting to return to spread more chaos, they shall instead be whisked away to another, less advanced planet, to live among those who are on a lower level. Imagine dying after residing in a beautiful mansion by the sea, bought by systematically stealing the wealth of others, then landing into the midst of a sewer smelling city, no modern technology, where luxury is having hot water boiled for you once a week. This is the punishment awaiting all who resist modifying their behavior and attitudes that celebrate robbing innocents, violence and feeling superior to those that don't stoop to their level. Even then, under God's benevolence, they too, shall have a chance to redeem themselves and re-ascend to a better planet.

The weeding out of the reluctant spirits and the populating of the planet with good spirits will be a gradual conversion. We are being groomed to attain the state required for us to inhabit a non-expiratory world. In *Genesis*, the Apocalypse will not occur in a big bang but will be; "According to the Spirits the earth will not be transformed by a cataclysm that will suddenly wipe out an entire generation. The current generation will disappear gradually and the new one will follow it in the same way, without there have been any change in the natural order of things."[233]

So what happens to us who remain? The Spirit of Truth, as promised in the New Testament John 14:15-17, as the Consoler sent to Allan Kardec to reveal the Doctrine of Spiritism, tells us in *The Gospel According to Spiritism*, what will be:

> "The time is near for the fulfillment of those things proclaimed for the transformation of humankind. Blessed will be those who have worked in the Lord's field selflessly and with no other motive than charity! Their workdays will be paid a hundredfold more than what they expected. Blessed will be those who said to their fellow men and women, "Brothers and sisters, let us work together and combine our efforts so that the Master may find the work accomplished at his coming"; for the Master will say to them; "Come unto me, you who have been good servants, you who have known how to silence your jealousies and discords so that no harm will come to the work!"[234]

Our hundredfold reward will be life on a Regenerative planet. Where there is more good than evil and we can thrive in an environment relatively free of discord. With no fear of war or other violent ends. A place, a safe haven, to continue learning how we can progress to become a pure spirit.

# Chapter 29 - Future of the Earth as Foretold by Spiritism

We have explained the process of the Apocalypse. A gradual thinning out of the undesirable element. So, where exactly are we going, and why should we fight for the right to be there?

Everyone is interested in the future. Well, it has all been mapped out. The endgame is known, the timing on how we get there is still a mystery, but it will come. All has been told to us in Allan Kardec's *The Spirits Book* and in books psychographed by Francisco C. Xavier. This chapter will take you through the major prophecies and what we can expect and how they will affect us.

Within the world of Spiritism, there are several main sources to understand what the Spirit world has in store for us. The fountainhead of all glimpses of the future starts with Allan Kardec's *The Spirits Book* and *Genesis*. They tell us of the ultimate goal for earth. The transition from an expiratory planet (a place where we are learning and paying for our sins) to regenerative planet (where we are still learning, but life is more conducive to harmony and painful periods are balanced by periods of rest and happiness). The tactics and strategy for how this is accomplished are covered in Francisco C. Xavier's books, mainly in the book *On the Way to the Light*, by the spirit Emmanuel.

First, let's look at how the Spirit World looks at our planet. In the book *Renunciation*, dictated by the spirit Emmanuel to Francisco Xavier, a woman spirit (Alcyone) has decided to return to earth to assist her love, who has not progressed. She currently resides in a different part of the galaxy, Sirius, where she is asking for transport back to Earth, to be physically reincarnated once more. She enters the room to be transported and an official says:

"Who is the traveler who is going to the **Dark Realms**?"

"Alcyone. She has offered her services for further work among incarnate spirits on Earth."

"What?" he asked, taken aback. "Alycone is going to drink the bitter cup of renunciation again?"[235]

The "Dark Realms" is not a marketer's idea of a description for an attractive vacation spot. It is as if we are given a choice of where we would like to go on vacation, the travel agent would say, "Would you like to go to Brazil, and visit Rio de Janeiro, or to Afghanistan, and visit the destroyed monuments and be kidnapped by the Taliban". We have been tagged as an undesirable location by those who know of us and have no wish to visit. At least we know where we stand in the Universal order; low on the totem pole.

What are levels of the planets and where do we actually stand in the hierarchy?

## Categories of Inhabited Worlds

### Primitive Planet

A primitive world is just what it sounds like – primitive. Think, being lost in the Amazon or in New Guinea amongst cannibals. According to Allan Kardec's *The Gospel According to Spiritism*, "On the least evolved worlds, the beings that inhabit them are, to a certain extent, rudimentary. They have the human form but are devoid of any beauty. Their instincts are not tempered by any sentiment of refinement or benevolence, or by any notions of right or wrong. Brute force is the only law. With no industry or inventions, they spend life in conquest of food."[236] There are vague notions of a Supreme Being, but overall, human spirits who have just reincarnated are sent here to first learn the consequences of evil.

### World of Trial and Expiation

As written in the previous chapter, you are living on this world. There are three types of spirits who are residing on earth;

1. Spirits from Primitive worlds – They are on earth for an education, a chance to develop themselves through

contact with more-advanced spirits.

2. Semi-civilized spirits – Spirits that are indigenous to earth, who have evolved little by little through long centennial periods.

3. Spirits undergoing trials from other planets – These spirits have already lived on other worlds, from which they were banished because they persisted in evil, and because they were a cause of disturbance to the good inhabitants. They have been relegated to living for a time among less advanced spirits, and since they carry with them their developed intelligence and the seed of acquired knowledge, they have the mission of helping them advance. That is why punished spirits are found in the midst of the most intelligent peoples. Having more sensitivity, the miseries of life are bitterer to them because sufferings bruise them more deeply than they bruise the primitive peoples, whose moral sense is more obtuse.[237]

## Regenerative Planet

What is a "Regenerative Planet" like? There is an explanation in The Spirits Book:

"Thus, in worlds of higher degree that our earth, wars are unknown, because no one thinks of doing harm to his fellow-beings, and there is consequently no motive for hatred or discord. The foresight of their future, which is intuitive in the people of these worlds, and the sense of security resulting from a conscience void of remorse, cause them to look forward to death without fear, as being simply a process of transformation, the approach of which they perceive without the slightest uneasiness."[238]

Hence, a regenerative world, is one where spirits prepare themselves to transition from a planet of tests and atonements (our earth) to even higher worlds of spiritual purity. There is still evil present to remind us of past follies. At least our planet is on an upward trend. On our new regenerative world we will still have trials, to help us learn and grow, but we will not have to atone for our past mistakes. As in life, there is always another level to attain. The best news is that we will be free of the baser emotions of pride, envy, and hate.

## Happy Worlds

On Happy Worlds, we still retain our human form, although the senses are more acute. The body changes, as described in *The Gospel According to Spiritism*, "The specific lightness of the body enables rapid and easy locomotion; instead of dragging itself laboriously over the ground, it glides – so to speak – over the surface or sails through  the air with no other effort that that of the will, in the way in which angels are portrayed."[239] With the improvement in our bodies, the years of infancy and adolescent are shorter, while the average lifespan is much longer than on earth today.

Politically on such worlds, "relationships between nations are always friendly and are never disturbed by the ambition of dominating their neighbor, or by war, which is its consequence. There are no masters, slaves or privileges of birth; only moral and intellectual ascendancy establish the differences of conditions and confer supremacy. Authority is always respected, for it is conferred only on those who have merit and it is always exercised with justice."[240]

Hatred, jealousies and selfishness are not present. All feel a sense of fraternity and love, where the strong assist the weak. Possessions are in keeping with a person's intelligence and no one lacks their basic needs for living. From here, the next transition is to a purified spirit, who lives on a heavenly world.

## Heavenly or Divine Worlds

On a Heavenly or Divine world, there exists only pure spirits. There is no evil.

# Our Future – The Foundation

We have a baseline, we are living in a world of Trial and Expiation and the goal of the spirit world is to transition the earth to a Regenerative planet. We shall become a world where wars are unthinkable and free of pride, envy, and hate. This sounds impossible. First, all reality shows would be cancelled and whole industries wiped off the face of the planet. But think for a minute, how far we have come from days when the world was full of tribes, when the only law, was the law of survival.

Before we get to the future, let us look at the recent past. The Spirit world through the writings of the Spirit Emmanuel, who dictated the book, *On the Way to the Light*, to Francisco C. Xavier, explained the reasons for the major wars of the twentieth century. Essentially, Europe was the vehicle to incubate democracy and intellectual pursuits superior to that of other nations of the world. As always, the rule of action and re-action, caught up with the European nations and their violent history.

From the time of Ancient Greece, through the Roman Empire, and finally out of the Dark Ages, the nations of Europe advanced. Militarily, philosophy, and scientifically they were more development than the rest of the world. As the modern age appeared, Europe continued to advance its society and scientific areas, but as the 1900's approached, the continent was caught in competition to see who could build a bigger colonial empire. The Franco-Prussian war of 1870 was a precursor to the terrible devastation of World War I. During this time the old colonial powers saw their reach severely diminished. World War II finished off any further thoughts of building empires by the nations of Europe. From these events we can determine that the spirit world has continually strived for a society where all people partake in their governance and when those democratic or republican forms of government turned to despotism or aggressive and violent empire building, then these countries are slowly sapped of power by the machinations of our spirit overseers.

# Our Future - The Americas

The spirit world's vision could see the demise of Europe, therefore from the beginning of the discovery of the New World they started to plan for the future of the Americas. Emmanuel describes the plan to bring a fresh beginning to the new land:

> "All the spirits called together to organize future progress flocked to the hemisphere of the New World. Many of them had acquired the sense of fraternity and peace after many struggles on their former continent."[241]

The Americas were being set-up for a greater good and primed to be ready for the next defining advancement. In parallel with sympathetic souls reincarnating in the Americas, a group of distinguished philosophers in Europe, such as Voltaire, Rousseau, and Montesquieu would lead the new American society into the future. The writings of these wise men were welcomed and adapted by the British Colonies in North America. When England refused the concept of equal representation, the American colonies rebelled and gained independence. The United States Constitution became the model for many countries.

In South America, the former colonies of Spain declared their independence in 1816. Later in 1822, Brazil proclaimed their emancipation from Portugal. Emmanuel makes the interesting observation:

> "Attentive to the mission of the Brazilian people in the civilization to come, it is worth noting the efforts of the invisible plane in maintaining Brazil's territorial integrity while the rest of the continent was being split into smaller republics."[242]

The Spirit world has a definite plan for the Americas; Emmanuel describes the mission of the New World:

> "On that field of new and regenerative struggles, all spirits of good will could work for the advent of peace and fraternity for humanity's future, and for that reason, having in mind the forthcoming centuries, they defined the role of each region on

the new continents, placing the brain of the new civilization where today's United States is located in North America, and its heart in the abundant and welcoming lands of Brazil in South America. The former was to hold the material powers; the latter, the first fruits of the spiritual powers destined for the planetary civilization of the future."[243]

Hence, as the Spirit world has accomplished in the past, they are arranging key areas of the planet to lead the rest of the nations onto a path toward Spiritism. Where Brazil will supply the religious doctrine, which we are seeing presently, with the appearance of Chico Xavier and other notable mediums. Along with the emigration of Brazilians to the US to spread the word of Spiritism. More and more cities now have a Spiritist center ready to teach about the eternal doctrine.

While the United States, with its material prowess and the global reach of our cultural movies and TV distribution, shall invest enormous resources to ingrain the Spiritist Doctrine into our daily lives. How will this occur? As with most grand transitions on a planetary scale, it will coming rolling at us at less than glacial speed.

### The Transition

Actually, the transition has been occurring since mankind appeared on earth. It has always been planned to take us through the stages from primitive to one of atonement and now to regenerative. The flow is gradual and unstoppable. The New Testament foretold that a great division will be coming. Next Spiritism, brought the message that we are being prepared for the transition of the earth from an expiratory sphere to a higher level, where the good spirits are the majority of the planet. Allan Kardec, in his book *Genesis*, explains the implications of the final judgment, "Since the good must finally reign on the earth, it will be necessary to exclude spirits who are hardened in evil and who could bring trouble to it. God has already allowed them the time needed for their improvement; but when the time comes in which, through the moral progress of its inhabitants, the earth must ascend in the hierarchy of worlds, it will be off limits as a home for incarnates and discarnates who have not taken advantage of the teachings they have been in a position to receive there. They will be exiled to lowers worlds as formerly those of the Adamic races were exiled to the earth, and they will be replaced by better spirits".[244]

The weeding out of the reluctant spirits and the populating of the planet with good spirits will be a gradual conversion. We are being groomed to attain the state required for us to inhabit a non-expiratory world. In *Genesis*, the Apocalypse will not occur in a big bang but will be; "According to the Spirits the earth will not be transformed by a cataclysm that will suddenly wipe out an entire generation. The current generation will disappear gradually and the new one will follow it in the same way, without there have been any change in the natural order of things".[245]

Therefore, the process is and was happening all around us and is continual, from the first human discovering fire to the small gatherings of Spiritists. It is in God's design that this conversion occurs. And again in *Genesis*, according to the Spirit world; "When something is in God's designs, it must be accomplished one way or another. Men and women contribute to its execution, but no one is indispensable; otherwise, God would be at the mercy of God's creatures".[246]

————— •◆•◆• —————

# Chapter 30 – A Peak into How the Spirit World wants us to treat the Environment

There are hints at more details of what a regenerative world would look like in the books by Allan Kardec and Chico Xavier. There are passages that pertain to earth's environment.

The spirit world is vitally interested in the state of the earth. Whereas, they recognize that the human race would have to travel through a transition phase of industry, they are planning for us to start repairing the damage that we have done to the planet. The aim is to restore balance between our presence and our planet's well-being.

The spirit world expects us to be good stewards of our land. In books written by Chico Xavier, there are references to how we should behave toward the natural beauty that has been bestowed upon us. There are even allusions to the task of maintaining the globe in *The Spirits Book*:

> *536. Are the great phenomena of nature, those, which we consider as perturbations of the elements, due to fortuitous causes, or have they all a providential aim? "There is a reason for everything; nothing takes place without the permission of God." Have these phenomena always some reference to mankind?*

> "They have sometimes a direct reference to man; but they have often no other object than the re-establishment of the equilibrium and harmony of the physical forces of nature."[247]

Hence, the earth, like all things under God, is managed by his representatives in the spirit world. The Laws of Nature handles most instances, but there are always situations, just like in our lives, where spirits must be present to guide situations onto the correct path.

An example of this is alluded to in *The Messengers*, inspired by the spirit Andre Luiz and psychographed by Chico Xavier. Andre Luiz is with his mentor, Aniceto, as they walk in the fields outside of Rio de Janeiro. Andre notices many spiritual entities around, he asks why and Aniceto tells him:

> "Nature is an immense workshop for us too," Aniceto remarked. Pointing to the other spirits, he added, "The plant kingdom has many cooperators. Perhaps you didn't know that many individuals prepare themselves for their next reincarnation by working within these kingdoms of Nature. The work of the Creator is carried on everywhere, at every moment."[248]

The work to sustain our world is never ending. Nature exists to work in harmony with mankind. We are on this planet to use what nature gives us and to use it wisely for the benefit of all and subsequent generations. This doesn't mean that we should renounce all progress and live in primitive conditions like we did thousands of years ago.

For humans were put on the planet to progress and part of our upward climb from a planet of atonement to a planet of regeneration is the successful management of our natural resources. In *The Spirits Book* we are told that we must continue to advance and to not heed the call of luddites who wish us to travel back into the dark ages:

*781. Has man the power of arresting the march of progress?*

"No; but he has sometimes that of hindering it."

- *What is to be thought of the men who attempt to arrest the march of progress, and to make the human race go backwards?*

"They are wretched weaklings whom God will chastise; they will be overthrown by the torrent they have tried to arrest."[249]

Those fanatical environmentalists who would like to return our civilization to the beginning of fire are misdirected. Yes, they are right we need to manage our resources better, but there is no turning back. We have to improve enough to learn how to sufficiently produce for the people who currently live on our globe, while sustaining the environment.

## Plea for the Land

Aniceto, Andre's mentor in the book *The Messengers*, speaks to a collection of spirits in a field outside of Rio de Janeiro, about the need to husband our resources:

"Nature has waited for humankind to offer its cooperation and understanding. She has not only waited in hope; but also in great expectation that human beings will offer comprehension and nurturing. However, the natural environment continues to suffer oppression from different manifestations of human self-interest. God expects humanity to look beyond self-interest and embrace nature as partner and thus attain its purpose in the glory of divine love."[250]

Therefore, while the human race must produce for the good of all, we should pay back our debt to the earth. What we have taken, we should give back. Where we have disfigured, we should repair. And not literally, for we must extract minerals and other resources, but when we are finished do we need to abandon the land looking like a moon-scape? Do we need to pollute the water in the process of mining? Yes, these steps decrease profits, but at what costs in the long term. If a project that wishes to use the earth, can't be profitable without maintaining the cleanliness of the area and restoring it to a decent state, then the development should not be undertaken.

Aniceto discusses the attitude of the land owner further:

"Most landowners exploit the land without giving anything in return. While you are working hard in order to maintain the natural equilibrium, human society acts as a destructive machine. Human beings have plunged into all kinds of excesses, whether from the heart or the stomach, giving little

210

though to their debts to the natural environment."[251]

Note that Aniceto is talking to a group of spirits. Spirits that have been entrusted to care for the surface of the earth. The spirit world is actively involved in all aspects, not just directing us individually, not just planning the course of nations, but also in picking up after us. As we pick up after the thoughtless destruction of our children, the spirit world is following us and cleaning our messes. All the while, we count up the material gain that we made.

Aniceto, finishes his discourse on the effect of humans on nature with this plea to his assembled group of spirit workers:

> "Let's teach our friends that life is not an unending robbery, where plants use up the soil, animals destroy plants, and humans kill animals. It is, however, an unending exchange, which we will never disturb without suffering serious consequences. Let's not judge them, let's help them!"[252]

An "unending exchange" is the key phrase. Where we are able to gain the goods that we require in exchange for caring for nature. When we harvest, we plant, when we extract, we repair and create other uses for the land that we disturb. When we pollute, we clean and insure we leave the land in the manner where it can take care of itself.

### A Hint at the Future

During Aniceto's speech to the spirits who are managing the land, he talks about the cycle of land to plants to animals to humans in terms of our required nourishment. He points out the chemical process whereby the human race collects the daily energy to survive:

> "As we all know, no living creature could survive on Earth without nitrogen. Although humans move around in an ocean of nitrogen and breathe in approximately one thousand liters per day, they cannot absorb it directly from the air. For the time being, Creation has not provided for the development of cells in the human body which are capable of removing nitrogen

from the soil and fixing it, so that other being can be fed by it. Each grain of wheat is a blessing, and each fruit is a receptacle of sugar and albumin, loaded with indispensable nitrogen. All farming, and cattle ranches are nothing more than the organized and methodological search for this precious element. If humans could fix only a small part of the nitrogen that they take in daily, Earth would be transformed into a true spiritual paradise."[253]

Could this mean that sometime in the future, we shall be genetically altered to directly absorb nitrogen? Thereby revolutionizing the entire food chain? First let determine what we know today about nitrogen and plant growth, from the Colorado State University garden notes:

"Nitrogen is the one nutrient most often limiting plant growth. The need for nitrogen varies from plant to plant. For example, tomatoes and vine crops (cucumbers, squash, and melons) will put on excessive vine growth at the expense of fruiting with excess nitrogen. Whereas potatoes, corn, and cole crops (cabbage, broccoli, and cauliflower) are heavy feeders and benefit from high soil nitrogen levels. Bluegrass turf and many annuals also benefit from routine nitrogen applications. Trees and shrubs have a low relative need for soil nitrogen."[254]

Hence, from nitrogen, and various other minerals and compounds, comes our basic food groups, of vegetables, fruits, and cereals. The nitrogen required by plants is the nitrogen found in the soil, except for clover which is able to process nitrogen directly from the atmosphere. Therefore, if we can't adapt to gain nutrients from nitrogen in the air, then could plants be modified to do so?

All of this is to point out that the spirit world may certainly foresee genetic modifications in our and our food crops future. While people are rightly conservative about genetically modified food, it may be what is waiting for us all.

In The Spirits Book, there is mention of what is used for food in a more advanced world:

*710. In worlds in which the corporeal organizations of living beings is of a purer nature than in the earth, do these need food?*

"Yes; but their food is in keeping with their nature. Their aliments would not be substantial enough for your gross stomachs and, on the other hand, those beings could not digest your heavier food."[255]

It is not mentioned in the answer whether the more advanced beings have always consumed less dense food, or they evolved physically as well as spiritually to a superior position.

My guess is that the spirit world has a tired and tested formula to raise up races from primitive to atonement to more advanced worlds. With the advances in spirituality, come great technical progress which allows a partially physical transformation of the species of the planet.

Already we are talking about implants to boost our memory, plus other ideas which would have been considered to be impossible science fiction a little over fifty years ago.

As stated at the beginning of the book, no one can stop progress, it is the will of the spirit world. Therefore, it shall be done and we are along for the ride. Who knows what marvelous contraptions we will see in our next life?

# Chapter 31 - NDE – Near Death Experience - William H

William H had a heart attack in 2003 and soon found himself out of his body and taken to another place. The link to his full story is William H NDE on the NDERF.org website, which contains many interesting NDE stories.

He describes what occurred:

"My whole life, it turned out, had been practice for the moment of dying: my higher soul stepped forward, speaking reassuringly about how it had been through this so many times before. While my lower soul, this lifetime's personality, went mute in the face of the vast Unknown, my higher soul catapulted into It with one last sigh of joy and gratitude: What a glorious Creation!"[256]

Almost immediately William realizes that we all travel through multiple lives. Upon his near death experience he finally learns the truth, that we are all immortal souls, who are reborn on earth to learn to be better. Although, he calls it "my higher soul", what actually occurred is his perispirit detached from his physical body. His perispirit contains all of his memories of his previous lives. We are our perispirits, we only temporarily inhabit our physical bodies and rely on our organic brain for the time we are here on earth.

William then describes what he felt in his body made of energy:

"I was fully awake when I realized I was myself a sphere of communion. A sphere of aware light. Surrounded by an infinite number of other spheres of aware light.

As I experienced it, then, the Sphere of Universal Communion is an infinite space of aware light that is occupied by all the individual spheres of aware light that ever have or ever will exist. As if it were One Mind, occupied by all the individual

Ideas it ever has or ever will conceive. Or a timeless, limitless, Oversoul, occupied by all the individual souls that ever have or ever will enter the realm of time, space, and personality. As I said, I do not pretend to know what it's true name is, but the relation between the Whole and its parts — and between parts and parts — this I can still see with diamond clarity."[257]

All of us have a unique signature that radiates from our minds. Our thoughts are constantly transmitting, like a radio tower, out to all around us, which travels to the end of the universe. Conversely, we receive others wavelengths, which contains thoughts from intelligences that surround us. Hence, as William sees it, we do live in a "sphere of universal communion", in continuous communication and we live in that state thanks to the benevolence of God, the Oversoul, who created all and set the natural laws that we must follow.

Next William writes:

"Each of us, as an individual sphere of communion seems the embodiment of two complementary halves: Understanding and Memory. While Understanding seems the principal characteristic of the higher soul, Memory seems to be the principal characteristic of the lower soul. As I experienced it, Understanding is our individual portion of the limitless Knowledge of the One Soul, the evolving insight we possess into the Way of the One, our individual spark of immortality. Memory, on the other hand, is the accumulated impressions of all the lifetimes we recall, the sum of all the personalities we have yoked to our soul, our enduring storehouse of mortal treasures."[258]

William is a just a bit off in his interpretation. Your perispirit, which is connected to your body, retains the memories you create while in your physical body. Yes, William is correct that it is your organic mind which first stores the memory, but all of them are uploaded into your perispirit, where if you wish, you could recall in life like detail every second of your favorite recollections or every millisecond of your life. You may ask, why can't we recall memories from our past lives? Some young children do, when the ties between the perispirit and the brain is forming, but most grow out of it.

What we do retain, is our conscience and instinct. Therefore, listen to your conscience, it contains countless years of experience and attempts to direct us on the right path. Heed your instincts, again, our accumulation of lives should make us better aware of when our decisions are in question.

Lastly, when you do pass from your current life, your memories of past lives do not return immediately, rather, they come back slowly and you accustom yourself back to your "real" life as a spirit.

William also perceives the love of the beings around him:

"Other individual spheres of aware light, many of great depth of Understanding with the Memory of thousands of lifetimes, generously taught me lessons to bring back and make use of in this lifetime. Such, it seems, is the loving-kindness of our collective ancestors, who care so deeply that this era of transformation is one of metamorphosis and not one of atrophy."259

Love is what God wants us to radiate. This is why we must journey through lives filled with strife, to absorb the lessons required to allow us to love all in every circumstance. To feel what others have felt and to reach out to help whenever it is needed. William doesn't yet realize that this is God's plan and that in our solar system, Jesus is our loving Governor. He is the one who directs the destiny of the earth.

William takes what he has felt and found that it carries over to our world:

"Although it is much more difficult to perceive here than in the Sphere of Universal Communion, we are no less individual spheres of communion here than we are there. Once I had experienced what it feels like to recognize myself as a sphere of aware light in the bodiless state, I found I had become sensitive enough to perceive myself as that same sphere of communion here with a body. And sensitive enough to recognize that everyone else is a similar sphere of aware light, as well."[260]

While we reside in our cumbersome bodies, our abilities to truly identify with others, to share thoughts, emotions, and love is diminished, we all should recognize that all humans are spirits, in many different levels of perfection. It is our duty to assist others in their quest to become better. Sometimes that means helping and other times it could mean some tough love, so they will be able to understand the lesson they need to internalize here on earth.

# Chapter 32 – What Can You Do?

Has your life been altered by what you have read? Hopefully, the realization that you are an immortal soul, who is one tiny, but important part of our universe has permeated into your being. For you are not just an organism made up of cells, bacteria and viruses grouped into larger organs that are merely controlled by another mass, called your brain. All of that, is our temporary housing, a mere shell, our spacesuit for earth, so we may live in the dense environment and complete the tasks given us by mission control.

## Why we are being tested

As in science fiction movies, where the people on a mission are scrutinized down to the molecular level, their biometrics measured, and their attitudes inspected and evaluated, we too are subjected to the same type of inspection. For every thought is recorded and stored. Every action is analyzed; what was our thinking when we first thought of the idea, did we ignore suggestions from our conscience to not perform our deed, did we enjoy what we did afterwards or were we regretful and learned from it.

All of this is extremely daunting and goes against our instincts for privacy and freedom. We rejoiced when we were able to finally free ourselves of the bonds of childhood and exist on our own without interference from our parents or other relatives. As we gained early adulthood, we did look back and recognize the necessity for wiser beings to guide us. We knew we lacked the basic skills to survive in the real world. As much as we liked to think we knew it all as teenagers, upon reflection, we knew that we still had some molding to suffer through.

As an adult, you have power. Power to ruin other lives. Either by driving recklessly, causing financial ruin, emotionally destroy an innocent, countless other methods to wreak havoc. Society understands that parenting is a solemn and required duty, for if we left our children alone, we would live in a savage world. Full of chaos, where progress would be unknown.

Now, think about the power of a pure spirit. Meditate a moment if all of us had the skills of Jesus. Would we use his ability to love, educate, and heal or would we turn those gifts to our own selfish desires. Seduce who we desire, accumulate wealth, and destroy our enemies. The power of a pure spirit in the spirit world is a magnitude greater, able to sway minds with a single thought, move at the speed of thought throughout the universe. Affect matter by merely directing your mind. Would you allow anyone to possess that power? Of course not.

Only those who have lived through rigorous training and real-life experiences should be considered for that honor. Preparation that could span millions of years, honing skills to insure that such god-like command is completely and immutably for good.

Hence, we incur a price to attain ultimate supremacy. The cost is up to us to pay or not. This is where our free-will begins. We are free to fail every test and to remain at our current level for eternity, if we so choose. The only penalty is to maintain a cycle of life in one of the Celestial cities or the Umbra and then in a body, experiencing over and over what we have gone through before.

At any time, if you wish, you may decide to start up once again on the ladder to perfection. It is entirely your decision. To ascend, takes dedication and practice. It's not easy, if it was, the earth would be depopulated.

## How to Ascend

You have read where we are not on earth for just one life, but many. Each life adding more to our conscience and instincts. While we are imprinted with the complete set of Divine Laws, as we mature our conscience grows in its ability to comprehend the laws in ever increasing circumstances. Every new birth, we come armed with a better governor, analyzing and letting us know the advisability of each move we take. We increase our awareness of the danger signs ahead of us. We feel more deeply when we have done the wrong thing. We are more satisfied when we have committed a good deed.

The Natural Laws of God are implanted in us. They are part of every spirit. We have the right to ignore them, but they are always there and our conscience provides detailed interpretations for each code, each regulation in the pantheon of laws.

Therefore, we don't need books like the one I have written, we have no requirement for dogmas or rituals. The Bible is superfluous and all of the literature written by saints and others telling us how to behave and think aren't necessary. For we contain the complete code within us. We just don't listen.

This is why the Bible and other teachings are important. Not to expose a new set of divine laws, but to convince our minds, our emotions, our passions to reflect for a moment and listen to our conscience.

Our path to ascend is tattooed inside us. A mark we can never erase. The map to happiness and bliss is clearly defined. Each road sign is unambiguous. We only have to heed the directions supplied us. How many times have you read in the Bible, where Jesus said, "If anyone has ears to hear, let them hear." This is precisely what was meant. If you would just listen to what you are saying to yourself, you will know!

To ascend, listen, have ears to hear. Instead of rushing to work, help that old lady across the street. Instead of saying something mean about your co-worker, help them succeed. Instead of feeling sorry for yourself, bring someone else up from their troubles.

Sounds so easy and yet so difficult. I know, I fail numerous times per day. I agonize how I ignore my inner voice every day. How many times have I seen a person look confused or obviously in need of assistance, yet moved on as I was focused on my own problems? I am ashamed to admit, feeling that pang of envy as co-workers were promoted or even praised and I wasn't. How base I am! How utterly uncharitable I am capable of being.

Yet, instead of wallowing in my constant failures, I still try. All I ask for is a small improvement every day. One example of learning to be better is the example given to us by Socrates. As

Spiritist we need to control our thoughts and not speak ill of others. In fact, we should seek out times to speak well of others. Socrates gives a great lesson on gossip.

One day the great philosopher came upon an acquaintance, who ran up to him excitedly and said, "Socrates, do you know what I just heard about one of your students?"

"Wait a moment," Socrates replied. "Before you tell me, I'd like you to pass a little test. It's called the Test of Three."

"Test of Three?"

"That's correct," Socrates continued. "Before you talk to me about my student let's take a moment to test what you're going to say. The first test is Truth. Have you made absolutely sure that what you are about to tell me is true?"

"No," the man replied, "actually I just heard about it."

"All right," said Socrates. "So you don't really know if it's true or not. Now let's try the second test, the test of Goodness. Is what you are about to tell me about my student something good?"

"No, on the contrary..."

"So," Socrates continued, "you want to tell me something bad about him even though you're not certain it's true?"

The man shrugged, a little embarrassed.

Socrates continued, "You may still pass though because there is a third test – the filter of Usefulness. Is what you want to tell me about my student going to be useful to me?"

"No, not really..."

"Well," concluded Socrates, "if what you want to tell me is neither true, nor good, nor even useful, why tell it to me at all?"

## What to Work On

Let us break down the lesson given to us by Socrates to discern how we should start on the pathway to purification. First, the man running to spread gossip, should have listened to that little voice in his head and refrained from telling Socrates his gossip. He could have skipped an embarrassing lesson.

Not talking or performing actions that you know are wrong is the first step. Learn to take a deep breath and wait for the green light. On the other hand, when you know you should take action, don't surrender to your other passions and do nothing. Begin by modifying your activities.

Second, couldn't the man filter the gossip he was hearing in the first place? As others were gleefully exposing the folly of another, which of course we all love to do! He could have told himself, "Why am I listening to this drivel?" Shutting off the bad influence from the start is the most efficient method to start training your mind and thoughts.

Create habits for your brain. After all, you practice sports by repetitive actions, the same goes for your mind. As you train your body to not perform certain actions, such as in not getting off balance during a golf swing, train your mind to avoid and then completely overlook certain thoughts.

You can't stand people who dress a certain way? Then teach your mind to look at them with love and caring thoughts. Use the knowledge that they too are in the fight for redemption. Erase your negative attitude and replace it with a positive glow. Allow your mind to radiate love and comfort to all around you.

Thirdly, when the man was listening to others speak badly about an acquaintance, think and act as you believe a high spirit would. Gently remind others you are not interested in malicious gossip and retreat from the conversation. An example is more powerful than lecturing others on what is right. They know deep down. If you put yourself on a pedestal other will spend more time attempting to figure out how to being you down than examining the lesson at hand.

Be a living demonstration of the power of love and caring. Of fraternity and justice. When the time is appropriate, let others know how you came onto your current path. For many will wish to know. A calm, collected, and stress-free person will attract many.

Acting and behaving as an upright person, one who understands that every thought and deed is recorded and assessed, will, as time goes by, become easier and easier. Repetition makes habits that will not only last a lifetime, but many lifetimes. For as you behave, your spirit, through the filter of your perispirit absorbs your new stance. When you rise out of your temporary body, your spirit will be better for the time spent on earth.

Practice climbing that high cliff and look down at your life. Where have you been, where are you now and where are you going. Serenely assess what you have learned and what you need to improve. Look back at the tough lessons and thank God that you were given the opportunity to participate in that class that you so clearly needed. Know, in your heart, that whatever shape you are in now is but a moment of time. A grain of sand compared to your immortal journey. Use every gift given to you to climb up the ladder.

Over the grand scheme of your life, be happy, for you live in a world of atonement, not a primitive world. You are done with the first years of elementary education. You are being prepared to start learning the more intellectual instructions, for in a few more lifetimes, you shall have a chance to reside in a world of regeneration. A world less burden by the onslaught of destructive passions. A world in which you and your loved ones may prosper and be together in harmony.

# Your Exploration Continues . . .

Learn more about Spiritism in my blog at:
http://www.nwspiritism.com.

To assist you in understanding more about Spiritism, I have
written four other books.

- The Case for Reincarnation – Your Path to Perfection
- Spiritism 101 – The Third Revelation
- 7 Tenets of Spiritism – How They Impact Your Daily
  life
- What Really Happens During Near Death Experiences
  According to Spiritism – 12 NDEs Explained and
  Explored

In the next sections are the introductions to my books.

Join us on Facebook at: https://www.facebook.com/nwspiritism

Join our discussion group on Spiritism at:
https://www.facebook.com/groups/Spiritist/

Go to the source of Spiritism and read Allan Kardec's books. The
two I find most interesting are:

1. The Spirits Book

2. The Gospel According to Spiritism

Follow the life of the spirit Andre Luiz, psychographed by
Francisco C. Xavier as he rises to the celestial city of Nosso Lar
and he experiences different aspects of how the spirit realm loves
and guides us is one of the most satisfying reads in my life. There
are thirteen books in the series, only eleven in English at this time,
and I urge you to read all of them in order.

1. Nosso Lar

2. The Messengers

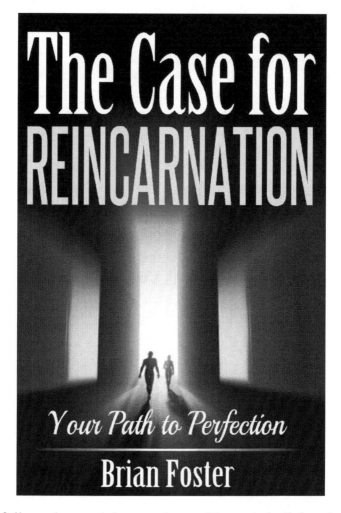

To fully understand the emotions of the people living through their NDEs and the actions of the spirit world in sending people back to earth, a review of how and why we travel through multiple lives is helpful.

You have lived multiple lives. At times you have been rich, poor, a servant and a slave. Maybe even a King or a Queen, at the least a member of the minor nobility.

Many famous people in the past have believed in reincarnation, such as Thomas Edison and Sir Arthur Conan Doyle. They both believed in the spirit world and made attempts to communicate with the world beyond.

There is a realm, a universe greater than ours and it is filled with intelligences that we can only wonder at. There are spirits around the earth who are actively helping and guiding us in our planning and during our actual incarnations.

You are interested in this book and in the topic because you know, in your heart that we are not merely chemical elements that dissolve with death. There must be something more, you know this, because of your own intuition, experiences and beliefs.

There are too many unexplained phenomena for there to be nothing after death. How do some people have past life memories? Why do children remember past lives and then lose the ability after a certain age? How can some people know the future? And more importantly, why do you have premonitions that come true? How could you know what could happen with such certainty?

Reincarnation is a tenet in many religions, such as Hinduism and Buddhism, and is frequently mentioned as parts of varied sects of Christianity and Judaism. It is the concept whereby we have a spirit, in which we retain our central personalities and memories, while in the spirit world, but lose our memories while in a physical form.

This book is here to answer your questions;

1. Why do we reincarnate?

2. How does the process work?

3. How many reincarnations must we have?

4. What memories do we retain from our previous lives?

5. Do we have control over our reincarnations?

6. Why must we suffer?

7. How may I insure my next life is better?

8. How may I progress to being a perfected spirit?

These questions are answered through the Doctrine of Spiritism. When, in the 1850's, the spirit world determine it was time for the human race to assimilate this knowledge in the hopes it would led us to understand the need to improve our spirituality and to achieve a better balance between our desire for material goods versus our desire to be a better person.

Explore what is your role and where you are in this journey. Determine your place and your future. Find out the reasons for your current tribulations and how to, not only survive your trials, but prosper through them.

Your journey in different bodies at different times in different circumstances is not without a purpose. You began as a primitive soul and through successive lives; you are being molded into a perfect spirit.

Dive deeper into all facets of reincarnation; my book is available at Amazon; *The Case for Reincarnation – Your Path to Perfection*

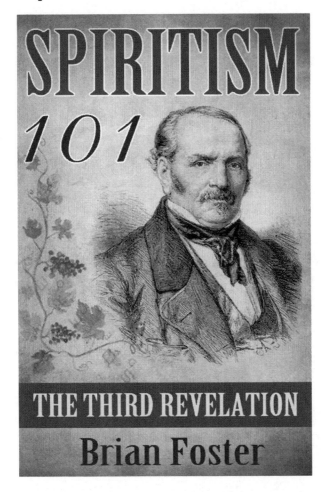

This short book is written as a review of the central concepts of the Doctrine of Spiritism.

### Introduction

Something wonderful has happened. It occurred in the middle of the 1800's and it caught the attention of the world. It grew quickly in popularity, so fast that many in positions of power went on a crusade to stamp it out.

Why? Because it provided answers to questions that we all have been searching for. Questions that have been posed by

229

philosophers since the beginning of time were asked and the results fully described.

Why such fear by the ruling religious classes? Because it explained the purpose for our life without dogma, without having to ask a priest or reverend for forgiveness. No special clothes to wear, no diet restrictions. No requirement for a specialized building or monthly stipends.

Why was it scorned? Because it didn't use the word "sin". It talked of spirits. It told us we could come back as either sex. And when it was asked about marriage, we were told that marriage is between two spirits, not two sexes.

We were told that a marriage should be the union of two spirits for as long as they work together in harmony. If not, then it wasn't the spirit world that stopped people from parting, it was our erroneous human convictions.

The organized Christian religions reacted strongly. They burned books and harassed those that knew and cherished the fact that the Third Revelation had occurred.

Like other messages of love, charity and fraternity before; this one was met with strong opposition. Ideas are hard to stamp out and this one is growing again. The world is re-awakening to Spiritism.

Learn what Spiritism is and how it can positively shape your life and happiness.

Available at Amazon Kindle and in paperback for - *Spiritism 101 – The Third Revelation*

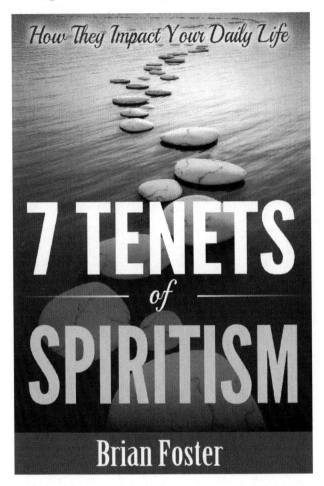

What are the seven tenets? They are the essential fluid and air in which we swim, walk and run in our daily lives. The seven tenets explain why your life is the way it is and how by realizing the Divine Force that surrounds us is a force for love, you can surmount any obstacle and withstand any ill wind.

Not only survive but prosper. For that is why we are here on earth. To learn, to improve, and to gain experiences. To place in the bottom of your heart that love, understanding, caring and serving are the tools we should use to solve every situation.

Sounds easy but in practice it's difficult. Everyday life swirls constantly around us, as if we live in an eye of a hurricane, and every misstep buffets our emotions. Life is a constant hardship for many. We need to rise above the terrain and visualize the road ahead. From the ground it looks rough and rocky, but from on-high the path appears smooth and the destination closer.

I explore each of the seven tenets and how they have personally affected me and those around me. How they will alter your view of your life and change your outlook and priorities. Giving yourself the seven tenets could be the best present of your life.

The 7 Tenets of Spiritism:

1. We are Immortal Souls

2. God and Jesus Love Us

3. We have Multiple Lives

4. During our Lives We Pay for Past Debts and Accumulate New Experiences

5. We Live and Learn in Close Family Groups

6. Our Destiny is Mostly Predetermined

7. We are Assisted in our Lives by Unseen Spirit Forces

Available at Amazon Kindle in in paperback.

# What Really Happens During Near Death Experiences, According to Spiritism

## 12 NDE's Explained and Explored

Why are we interested in Near Death Experiences (NDE)? With the advent of the internet, social media allows masses of people to more efficiently pool together shared experiences than at any other time in history. What was once an isolated phenomenon is now a common occurrence. Whereas, in times past a simple farmer or a rich landowner who would be able to pull back from death, their story, if they chose to tell it, would be a solitary happenstance. Easily explained away or believed. It made no difference, since the significance of the account would be eventually dismissed as an outlying data point.

The recent improvement in the speed and efficiency of human

communication in conjunction with modern medical methods of assisting the human body to recover after trauma has supported the explosion of accounts. And as the interpretations of each individual who returned became widely known and disseminated, others choose to finally reveal their own personal story.

Therefore a small bookshelf of NDEs is now becoming a library. Recollections from every country, culture, language and age group now reside in the great internet cloud. A mountain of data, which can no longer be wished away or ignored. The parallels and common themes from all corners of the world preclude everyone's account to be merely mass hysteria. NDEs aren't in the territory of alien encounters. Doctors, lawyers, professors, engineers, sales and service people are reporting in. Telling us similar refrains, with the added mystery of some NDEs where the person either saw or is told of events that they could not have possibly known in their current state. Taken as a whole, the only conclusion is that something must be happening, beyond our comprehension.

What Really Happens During Near Death Experiences – 12 NDEs Explained and Explored is available at Amazon.

# Author

Stay in touch with the author via:

Spiritist Blog: http://www.nwspiritism.com

Facebook: https://www.facebook.com/nwspiritism

Facebook group to discuss Spiritism: (please request to join)
https://www.facebook.com/groups/Spiritist/

Twitter: https://twitter.com/nwspiritism

If you liked *Explore Your Destiny – Since Your Life's Path is (mostly) Predetermined*, please post a review at Amazon.

# Copyright

# Bibliography

Amazon. (2014, May 11). *Genesis*. Retrieved from Amazon
    Books: http://www.amazon.com/Genesis-Miracles-
    Predictions-According-
    Spiritism/dp/8598161780/ref=sr_1_11?s=books&ie=UTF8
    &qid=1399825900&sr=1-11&keywords=allan+kardec

Amazon. (2014, May 11). *Heaven and Hell*. Retrieved from
    Amazon Books: http://www.amazon.com/Heaven-Hell-
    Allan-
    Kardec/dp/8598161349/ref=sr_1_8?s=books&ie=UTF8&qi
    d=1399825900&sr=1-8&keywords=allan+kardec

Amazon. (2014, May 11). *The Mediums Book*. Retrieved from
    Amazon Books: http://www.amazon.com/Mediums-Book-
    Allan-
    Kardec/dp/8598161829/ref=sr_1_5?s=books&ie=UTF8&qi
    d=1399825900&sr=1-5&keywords=allan+kardec

Amazon. (2014, May 14). *The Spirits Book*. Retrieved from
    Amazon Books: http://www.amazon.com/Spirits-Book-
    Spiritualist-
    Classics/dp/1907355987/ref=sr_1_1?s=books&ie=UTF8&
    qid=1399825900&sr=1-1&keywords=allan+kardec

Best of Sherlock. (2014, Dec. 20). *Best of Sherlock - Top 10
    Quotes*. Retrieved from Best of Sherlock:
    http://www.bestofsherlock.com/top-10-sherlock-
    quotes.htm#impossible

Colorado State University. (2014, October 11). *CMG Garden
    Notes*. Retrieved from Colorado State University Extension
    classes:
    http://www.ext.colostate.edu/mg/gardennotes/231.html

Denis, L. (2012). *Life and Destiny*. Forgotten Books.

Dias, H. D. (2014, Dec. 23). *Seminário Apocalipse, Mitos e
    Verdades com Haroldo Dutra Dias_1ª parte*. Retrieved

from YouTube:
https://www.youtube.com/watch?v=4SU2b11IbMg

Dictionary.com. (2014, 03 02). *Dictionary Reference*. Retrieved
from Dictionary.com:
http://dictionary.reference.com/browse/didactic

E., N. (2014, Dec. 20). *Nicola E Friend Other*. Retrieved from
NDERF.org:
http://www.nderf.org/NDERF/NDE_Experiences/nicola_e_
friend_other.htm

Ellis, M. (Dec., 26 2014). *blog.godreports*. Retrieved from God
Reports: http://blog.godreports.com/2012/03/atheist-
professors-near-death-experience-in-hell-left-him-changed/

G., D. (2014, August 1). *NDE Experiences - David G. ADC*.
Retrieved from NDERF.org:
http://www.nderf.org/NDERF/NDE_Experiences/david_g_
adc.htm

Hooper, R. (2007, 2012). *Jesus, Buddha, Krishna & Lao Tzu*. New
York: Bristol Park Books.

Kardec, A. (2006). *Heaven and Hell*. Brasilia (DF), Brasil:
International Spiritist Council.

Kardec, A. (2008). *The Gospel According to Spiritism*. Brasilia
(DF): International Spiritist Council.

Kardec, A. (2009). *Genesis - Miracles and Predictions according
to Spiritism*. Brasilia (DF), Brasil: International Spiritist
Council.

Kardec, A. (2010). *The Spirits Book*. Guildford, UK: White Crow
Books.

NDERF. (2014, Dec. 31). *WIlliam H NDE*. Retrieved from
NDERF - Near Death Experience Research Foundation:
http://www.nderf.org/NDERF/NDE_Experiences/william_
h_nde_7340.htm

NDERF. (2015, January 12). *Ronnie D NDE*. Retrieved from Near Death Experiences Research Foundation: http://www.nderf.org/NDERF/NDE_Experiences/ronnie_d_nde.htm

NDERF.org. (2015, Jan. 3). *Amy C Near Death Experience 4720*. Retrieved from nderf.org: http://www.nderf.org/NDERF/amy_c_nde_4720.htm

NDERF.org. (2015, Feb. 7). *Romy NDE*. Retrieved from NDERF.org: http://www.nderf.org/NDERF/NDE_Experiences/romy_nde.htm

Near Death Experience Research Foundation. (2014, Dec. 13). *NDERF - Anna A*. Retrieved from NDERF: http://www.nderf.org/NDERF/NDE_Experiences/anna_a_nde.htm

Near Death Experience Research Foundation. (2014, June 28). *NDERF - Gail*. Retrieved from NDERF: http://www.nderf.org/NDERF/NDE_Archives/NDERF_NDEs.htm

Near Death Experience Research Foundation. (2015, 2 1). *bronwen C NDE*. Retrieved from NDERF.org: http://www.nderf.org/NDERF/NDE_Experiences/bronwen_c_nde.htm

Near Death Experiences Research Foundation . (2015, Jan. 01). *Sara A Probable NDE*. Retrieved from NDERF.org: http://www.nderf.org/NDERF/NDE_Experiences/sara_a_probable_nde.htm

Neto, G. L. (2013, June 15). *Remembering Chico Xavier and His Legacy*. Retrieved from YouTube: https://www.youtube.com/watch?v=wY5m3bk0AsY&list=TL01TkXUPh4dbuxLuFJq7Gmn-QZpLdKa5H

Pereira, Y. A. (2012). *Memoirs of a Suicide*. Brasilia (DF), Brasil:

International Spiritist Council (EDICEI).

Spiritism. (n.d.). *Wikipedia - Spiritism*. Retrieved September 18, 2014, from Wikipedia: http://en.wikipedia.org/wiki/Spiritism

Steere, E. K. (2014, Oct. 6). *Research into Near Death Experiences Reveals Awareness May Continue even After the Brain Shutrs Down*. Retrieved from Daily Mail: http://www.dailymail.co.uk/health/article-2783030/Research-near-death-experiences-reveals-awareness-continue-brain-shut-down.html

Swedenborg, E. (1758). *Heaven and Hell*. Europe: A Publice Domain Book.

Swedenborg, E. (2011). *A Swedenborg Sampler*. West Chester, PA: Swedenborg Foundation Press.

Wikipedia. (2014, March 7). *Allan Kardec*. Retrieved from Wikipedia: http://en.wikipedia.org/wiki/Allan_Kardec

Wikipedia. (2014, Dec. 24). *Bezerra de Menezes*. Retrieved from pt.Wikipedia (Portuguese): http://pt.wikipedia.org/wiki/Bezerra_de_Menezes

Wikipedia. (2014, August 21). *Camilo Castelo Branco*. Retrieved from Wikipedia: http://en.wikipedia.org/wiki/Camilo_Castelo_Branco

Wikipedia. (2014, March 7). *Chico Xavier*. Retrieved from Wikipedia: http://en.wikipedia.org/wiki/Chico_Xavier

Wikipedia. (2014, December 23). *Henry the Navigator*. Retrieved from Wikipedia: http://en.wikipedia.org/wiki/Henry_the_Navigator

Wikipedia. (2014, June 26). *Wikipedia - Emanuel Swedenborg*. Retrieved from Wikipedia: http://en.wikipedia.org/wiki/Emanuel_Swedenborg

Wikipedia. (2014, 11 22). *Wikipedia - Golden Rule*. Retrieved from Wikipedia: http://en.wikipedia.org/wiki/Golden_Rule

Wikipedia. (2015, January 12). *Sleep Paralysis*. Retrieved from Wikipedia: http://en.wikipedia.org/wiki/Sleep_paralysis

Wikipedia. (n.d.). *Wikipedia - Arthur Conan Doyle*. Retrieved September 20, 2014, from Wikipedia: http://en.wikipedia.org/wiki/Arthur_Conan_Doyle

Wikipedia. (n.d.). *Wikipedia - Carl Jung*. Retrieved September 20, 2014, from Wikipedia: http://en.wikipedia.org/wiki/Carl_Jung#Spirituality

Wikipedia. (n.d.). *Wikipedia - Carl Wickland*. Retrieved September 20, 2014, from Wikipedia: http://en.wikipedia.org/wiki/Carl_Wickland

Wikipedia. (n.d.). *Wikipedia - Subtle Body*. Retrieved September 20, 2014, from Wikipedia: http://en.wikipedia.org/wiki/Subtle_body

Wikipedia. (n.d.). *Wikipedia - Synchronicity*. Retrieved September 22, 2014, from Wikipedia: http://en.wikipedia.org/wiki/Synchronicity

Xavier, F. C. (2004). *In the Domain of Mediumship*. New York: Spiritist Alliance of Books, Inc.

Xavier, F. C. (2008). *The Messengers*. Philadelphia, PA: Allan Kardec Educational Society.

Xavier, F. C. (2008). *Workers of the Life Eternal*. Brasilia (DF) - Brazil: International Spiritist Council.

Xavier, F. C. (2009). *And Life Goes On*. Brasilia (DF), Brasil: International Spiritist Council.

Xavier, F. C. (2009). *In the Greater World*. Brasilia (DF), Brazil: International Spiritist Council.

Xavier, F. C. (2009). *Missionaries of the Light*. Brasilia (DF),

Brazil: International Spiritist Council.

Xavier, F. C. (2010). *Action and Reaction.* Brasilia (DF), Brazil: International Spiritist Council.

Xavier, F. C. (2010). *Nosso Lar.* Brasilia - (DF), Brazil: International Spiritist Council.

Xavier, F. C. (2011). *Between Heaven and Earth.* Brasilia (DF), Brazil: International Spiritist Council.

Xavier, F. C. (2011). *In the Realms of Mediumship.* Brasilia (DF), Brazil: EDICEI.

Xavier, F. C. (2011). *On the Way to the Light.* Brasilia (DF), Brazil: International Spiritist Council.

Xavier, F. C. (2013). *Liberation.* Brasilia (DF), Brazil: International Spiritist Council.

Xavier, F. C. (2013). *Sex and Destiny.* Miami, FL: EDICEI of America.

[1] en.wikipedia.org/wiki/Chico_Xavier
[2] en.wikipedia.org/wiki/Allan_Kardec
[3] www.nderf.org
[4] www.nderf.org
[5] www.nderf.org
[6] www.near-death.com/experiences/reincarnation02.html
[7] Kardec, Allan. The Spirits Book, White Crow Books Questions 154,155, pp. 134-135
[8] Kardec, Allan. Heaven and Hell, EDICEI Cap. 2, items 7-8
[9] Xavier, Francisco C. Workers of the Life Eternal, EDICEI, p. 267
[10] XAVIER, Francisco C. Between Heaven and Earth, EDICEI, p. 79
[11] nderf.org, Individual NDE experiences:, n.d., http://www.nderf.org/NDERF/NDE_Archives/NDERF_NDEs.htm (accessed May 16, 2014)
[12] XAVIER, Francisco C. The Messengers, Allan Kardec Educational Society, p. 52
[13] XAVIER, Francisco C. The Messengers, Allan Kardec Educational Society, p. 53
[14] KARDEC, Allan The Gospel According to Spiritism, EDICEI, Chap. V, Item 11, p. 103
[15] KARDEC, Allan The Gospel According to Spiritism, EDICEI, Chap. V, Item 11, p. 103
[16] KARDEC, Allan. The Gospel According to Spiritism, EDICEI Cap. 5, item 4
[17] XAVIER, Francisco C. Missionaries of the Light, EDICEI, p. 225
[18] XAVIER, Francisco C. Missionaries of the Light, EDICEI p. 225
[19] XAVIER, Francisco C. Missionaries of the Light, EDICEI p. 226
[20] XAVIER, Francisco C. Missionaries of the Light, EDICEI p.

226

[21] XAVIER, Francisco C. Action and Reaction, EDICEI p. 88

[22] XAVIER, Francisco C. Action and Reaction, EDICEI p. 89

[23] XAVIER, Francisco C. Action and Reaction, EDICEI p. 90

[24] NDERF.org, "My NDE", n.d., http://nhneneardeath.ning.com/profiles/blogs/my-nde-2, (accessed Sept. 6, 2014)

[25] NDERF.org, "My NDE", n.d., http://nhneneardeath.ning.com/profiles/blogs/my-nde-2, (accessed Sept. 6, 2014)

[26] Pereira, Y. A., Memoirs of a Suicide, EDICEI, p. 424

[27] Xavier, F.C., Missionaries of the Light, EDICEI, p. 179

[28] NDERF.org, "My NDE", n.d., http://nhneneardeath.ning.com/profiles/blogs/my-nde-2, (accessed Sept. 6, 2014)

[29] Kardec, A., The Spirits Book, Guildford, UK, White Crow Books, Chap. 4, ques. 166, p. 141

[30] XAVIER, Francisco C. Workers of the Lifer Eternal, Brasilia (DF),EDICEI, p. 365

[31] dictionary.reference.com/browse/didactic

[32] XAVIER, Francisco C. Workers of the Lifer Eternal, Brasilia (DF), EDICEI, p. 365

[33] Kardec, A., The Spirits Book, Guildford, UK, White Crow Books, Chap. 4, ques. 175, p. 144

[34] Kardec, A., The Spirits Book, Guildford, UK, White Crow Books, Chap. 4, ques. 172-173, pp. 143-144

[35] Kardec, A., The Gospel According to Spiritism, Brasilia (DF), EDICEI, Chap. 3, Sect. 17, p. 76

[36] Denis, L., Life and Destiny, Forgotten Books, p. 208

[37] Denis, L., Life and Destiny, Forgotten Books, p. 208

[38] Denis, L., Life and Destiny, Forgotten Books, p. 208

[39] Pereira, Y. A., Memoirs of a Suicide, EDICEI, p. 8

[40] Wikipedia, "Leon Denis", n.d., http://en.wikipedia.org/wiki/Leon_Denis (accessed June 6, 2014)

[41] Pereira, Y. A., Memoirs of a Suicide, EDICEI, p. 270

[42] Pereira, Y. A., Memoirs of a Suicide, EDICEI, pp. 270-271

[43] Pereira, Y. A., Memoirs of a Suicide, EDICEI, p. 271

[44] Xavier, Francisco C., In the Realms of Mediumship, EDICEI, pp. 8-9

[45] Xavier, Francisco C., In the Realms of Mediumship, EDICEI, p. 9

[46] Xavier, Francisco C., In the Realms of Mediumship, EDICEI, p. 14

[47] Xavier, Francisco C., In the Realms of Mediumship, EDICEI, p. 20

[48] Xavier, Francisco C., In the Realms of Mediumship, EDICEI, p. 21

[49] Xavier, Francisco C., In the Realms of Mediumship, EDICEI, p. 22

[50] Xavier, Francisco C., In the Realms of Mediumship, EDICEI, pp. 23-24

[51] Xavier, Francisco C., In the Realms of Mediumship, EDICEI, p. 25

[52] Xavier, Francisco C., In the Realms of Mediumship, EDICEI, p. 26

[53] XAVIER, Francisco C. In the Greater World, EDICEI, p. 16

[54] XAVIER, Francisco C. In the Greater World, EDICEI, p. 17

[55] XAVIER, Francisco C. In the Greater World, EDICEI, p. 23

[56] XAVIER, Francisco C. In the Greater World, EDICEI, p. 27

[57] XAVIER, Francisco C. In the Greater World, EDICEI, p. 30

[58] XAVIER, Francisco C. In the Greater World, EDICEI, p. 31

[59] XAVIER, Francisco C. In the Greater World, EDICEI, p. 31

[60] Kardec, Allan, Genesis, EDICEI, p. 428

[61] Kardec, Allan, Genesis, EDICEI, p. 429

[62] www.merriam-webster.com/dictionary/innate

[63] XAVIER, Francisco C. In the Greater World, EDICEI, p. 31

[64] XAVIER, Francisco C. In the Greater World, EDICEI, p. 33

[65] XAVIER, Francisco C. In the Greater World, EDICEI, p. 32

[66] XAVIER, Francisco C. In the Greater World, EDICEI, p. 201

[67] XAVIER, Francisco C. In the Greater World, EDICEI, p. 204

[68] XAVIER, Francisco C. In the Greater World, EDICEI, p. 205

[69] XAVIER, Francisco C. In the Greater World, EDICEI, p. 208

[70] Denis, L., Life and Destiny, Forgotten Books, p. 207

[71] Denis, L., Life and Destiny, Forgotten Books, p. 207

[72] Xavier, F.C. Missionaries of the Light, EDICEI, pp. 217-218
[73] Xavier, F.C. Missionaries of the Light, EDICEI, pp. 219-220
[74] Xavier, F.C. Missionaries of the Light, EDICEI, pp. 154-155
[75] Xavier, F.C. Action and Reaction, EDICEI, pp. 210-211
[76] Xavier, F.C. Action and Reaction, EDICEI, p. 211
[77] Xavier, F.C. Sex and Destiny, EDICEI, p. 289
[78] Xavier, F.C. Sex and Destiny, EDICEI, p. 315
[79] Xavier, F.C. Sex and Destiny, EDICEI, pp. 318-319
[80] Xavier, F.C. Missionaries of the Light, EDICEI, pp. 326-327
[81] Xavier, F.C. Missionaries of the Light, EDICEI, p. 327
[82] Xavier, F.C. Missionaries of the Light, EDICEI, p. 327
[83] Xavier, F.C. Missionaries of the Light, EDICEI, p. 328
[84] Xavier, F.C. Missionaries of the Light, EDICEI, p. 329
[85] Xavier, F.C. Missionaries of the Light, EDICEI, p. 322
[86] Xavier, F.C. Missionaries of the Light, EDICEI, p. 324
[87] Xavier, F.C. Missionaries of the Light, EDICEI, pp. 334-335
[88] Xavier, F.C. Missionaries of the Light, EDICEI, p. 335
[89] NDERF.org, "Michael Joseph NDE", n.d.,
http://www.nderf.org/NDERF/NDE_Experiences/michael_joseph_
nde.htm, (accessed Aug. 8, 2014)
[90] NDERF.org, "Michael Joseph NDE", n.d.,
http://www.nderf.org/NDERF/NDE_Experiences/michael_joseph_
nde.htm, (accessed Aug. 8, 2014)
[91] NDERF.org, "Michael Joseph NDE", n.d.,
http://www.nderf.org/NDERF/NDE_Experiences/michael_joseph_
nde.htm, (accessed Aug. 8, 2014)
[92] NDERF.org, "Michael Joseph NDE", n.d.,
http://www.nderf.org/NDERF/NDE_Experiences/michael_joseph_
nde.htm, (accessed Aug. 8, 2014)
[93] NDERF.org, "Michael Joseph NDE", n.d.,
http://www.nderf.org/NDERF/NDE_Experiences/michael_joseph_
nde.htm, (accessed Aug. 8, 2014)
[94] Xavier, Francisco C., In the Realms of Mediumship, EDICEI,
p. 9
[95] Wikipedia, "Golden Rule", n.d,
http://en.wikipedia.org/wiki/Golden_Rule, (accessed November
22, 2014)

[96] Wikipedia, "Allan Kardec", n.d., http://en.wikipedia.org/wiki/Allan_Kardec, (accessed May 10, 2014)

[97] Wikipedia, "Allan Kardec", n.d., http://en.wikipedia.org/wiki/Allan_Kardec, (accessed May 10, 2014)

[98] Spirit Writings, "Allan Kardec Biography:, n.d., http://www.spiritwritings.com/kardec.html (accessed May 10, 2014)

[99] Spirit Writings, "Allan Kardec Biography:, n.d., http://www.spiritwritings.com/kardec.html (accessed May 10, 2014)

[100] Spirit Writings, "Allan Kardec Biography:, n.d., http://www.spiritwritings.com/kardec.html (accessed May 10, 2014)

[101] Amazon, "The Spirits Book", n.d., http://www.amazon.com/Spirits-Book-Spiritualist-Classics/dp/1907355987/ref=sr_1_1?s=books&ie=UTF8&qid=1399825900&sr=1-1&keywords=allan+kardec (accessed May 11, 2014)

[102] Amazon, "The Mediums Book", n.d., http://www.amazon.com/Mediums-Book-Allan-Kardec/dp/8598161829/ref=sr_1_5?s=books&ie=UTF8&qid=1399825900&sr=1-5&keywords=allan+kardec (accessed May 11, 2014)

[103] Amazon, "The Gospel According to Spiritism", n.d., http://www.amazon.com/Gospel-According-Spiritism-Allan-Kardec/dp/8598161705/ref=sr_1_6?s=books&ie=UTF8&qid=1399825900&sr=1-6&keywords=allan+kardec (accessed May 11, 2014)

[104] Amazon, "Heaven and Hell",n.d., http://www.amazon.com/Heaven-Hell-Allan-Kardec/dp/8598161349/ref=sr_1_8?s=books&ie=UTF8&qid=1399825900&sr=1-8&keywords=allan+kardec (accessed May 11, 2014)

[105] Amazon, "Genesis", n.d., http://www.amazon.com/Genesis-Miracles-Predictions-According-Spiritism/dp/8598161780/ref=sr_1_11?s=books&ie=UTF8&qid=1399825900&sr=1-11&keywords=allan+kardec (accessed May 11,

2014)

[106] Kardec, A., The Gospel According to Spiritism, EDICEI, p. 20

[107] Kardec, A., The Gospel According to Spiritism, EDICEI, p. 22

[108] Kardec, A., The Gospel According to Spiritism, EDICEI, p. 23

[109] Kardec, A., The Gospel According to Spiritism, EDICEI, p. 25

[110] Kardec, A., The Gospel According to Spiritism, EDICEI, p. 27

[111] Wikipedia, "Chico Xavier", n.d., http://en.wikipedia.org/wiki/Chico_Xavier, (accessed May 4, 2014)

[112] Neto, G. L. Remembering Chico Xavier and His Legacy, YouTube, (accessed May 3, 2014)

[113] Wikipedia, "Chico Xavier", n.d., http://en.wikipedia.org/wiki/Chico_Xavier, (accessed May 4, 2014)

[114] Wikipedia, "Chico Xavier", n.d., http://en.wikipedia.org/wiki/Chico_Xavier, (accessed May 4, 2014)

[115] Wikipedia, "Chico Xavier", n.d., http://en.wikipedia.org/wiki/Chico_Xavier, (accessed May 4, 2014)

[116] Neto, G. L. Remembering Chico Xavier and His Legacy, YouTube, (accessed May 3, 2014)

[117] Neto, G. L. Remembering Chico Xavier and His Legacy, YouTube, (accessed May 3, 2014)

[118] Neto, G. L. Remembering Chico Xavier and His Legacy, YouTube, (accessed May 3, 2014)

[119] Wikipedia, "Socrates", n.d., http://en.wikipedia.org/wiki/Socrates, (accessed August 5, 2014)

[120] Wikipedia, "Socrates", n.d., http://en.wikipedia.org/wiki/Socrates, (accessed August 5, 2014)

[121] Kardec, A., The Gospel According to Spiritism, EDICEI, p. 42

[122] Wikipedia, "Socrates", n.d.,
http://en.wikipedia.org/wiki/Socrates, (accessed August 5, 2014)
[123] Kardec, A., The Gospel According to Spiritism, EDICEI, p. 43
[124] Kardec, A., The Gospel According to Spiritism, EDICEI, pp. 37-38
[125] Kardec, A., The Gospel According to Spiritism, EDICEI, p. 39
[126] Kardec, A., The Gospel According to Spiritism, EDICEI, p. 42
[127] Kardec, A., The Gospel According to Spiritism, EDICEI, p. 44
[128] Xavier, F.C. Workers of the Life Eternal, EDICEI, p 24
[129] Wikipedia, "Emanuel Swedenborg", n.d.,
http://en.wikipedia.org/wiki/Emanuel_Swedenborg (accessed June 26, 2014)
[130] Swedenborg, E. A Swedenborg Sampler, Swedenborg Foundation Press, p ix
[131] Swedenborg, E. A Swedenborg Sampler, Swedenborg Foundation Press, p xi
[132] Swedenborg, E. A Swedenborg Sampler, Swedenborg Foundation Press, p xii
[133] Swedenborg, E. A Swedenborg Sampler, Swedenborg Foundation Press, p xiv
[134] Swedenborg, E. A Swedenborg Sampler, Swedenborg Foundation Press, p xiv
[135] Swedenborg, E. A Swedenborg Sampler, Swedenborg Foundation Press, p xiv
[136] Swedenborg, E. A Swedenborg Sampler, Swedenborg Foundation Press, p 10
[137] Swedenborg, E. A Swedenborg Sampler, Swedenborg Foundation Press, p 27
[138] Swedenborg, E. A Swedenborg Sampler, Swedenborg Foundation Press, p 32
[139] Wikipedia, "Methodism", n.d.,
http://en.wikipedia.org/wiki/Methodism (accessed June 28, 2014)
[140] Wikipedia, "Emanuel Swedenborg", n.d.,

http://en.wikipedia.org/wiki/Emanuel_Swedenborg (accessed June 28, 2014)

[141] Wikipedia, "Emanuel Swedenborg", n.d., http://en.wikipedia.org/wiki/Emanuel_Swedenborg (accessed June 28, 2014)

[142] Wikipedia, "Emanuel Swedenborg", n.d., http://en.wikipedia.org/wiki/Emanuel_Swedenborg (accessed June 28, 2014)

[143] Wikipedia, "Emanuel Swedenborg", n.d., http://en.wikipedia.org/wiki/Emanuel_Swedenborg (accessed June 28, 2014)

[144] KARDEC, Allan, The Spirits Book, White Crow Books, Question 1012, p. 519

[145] Xavier, Francisco C., Liberation, EDICEI, p. 106

[146] Xavier, Francisco C., Liberation, EDICEI, p. 57

[147] Xavier, Francisco C., Liberation, EDICEI, p. 63

[148] Xavier, Francisco C., Liberation, EDICEI, p. 67

[149] Xavier, Francisco C., Liberation, EDICEI, p. 59

[150] Xavier, Francisco C., Liberation, EDICEI, p. 218

[151] Holy Bible, pp. MT 25:31-34

[152] KARDEC, Allan. Genesis, EDICEI Cap. 16, item 63

[153] KARDEC, Allan. Genesis, EDICEI Cap. 18, item 27

[154] KARDEC, Allan. Genesis, EDICEI Cap. 16, item 13

[155] KARDEC, Allan. Genesis, EDICEI Cap. 16, item 13

[156] Holy Bible, pp. EP 1:9-11

[157] Holy Bible, pp. GA 1: 15-16

[158] XAVIER, Francisco C. On the Way to the Light, EDICEI, p. 123

[159] XAVIER, Francisco C. On the Way to the Light, EDICEI, p. 193

[160] Wikipedia - http://en.wikipedia.org/wiki/Monte_Carlo_method

[161] XAVIER, Francisco C. On the Way to the Light, EDICEI, p. 92

[162] XAVIER, Francisco C. On the Way to the Light, EDICEI, p. 138

[163] XAVIER, Francisco C. On the Way to the Light, EDICEI, p.

123
[164] XAVIER, Francisco C. On the Way to the Light, EDICEI, p. 167
[165] XAVIER, Francisco C. On the Way to the Light, EDICEI, p. 147
[166] XAVIER, Francisco C. On the Way to the Light, EDICEI, p. 155
[167] XAVIER, Francisco C. On the Way to the Light, EDICEI, p. 180
[168] XAVIER, Francisco C. Action and Reaction, EDICEI, p. 160
[169] XAVIER, Francisco C. Workers of the Life Eternal, EDICEI, p. 239
[170] XAVIER, Francisco C. Workers of the Life Eternal, EDICEI, p. 238
[171] KARDEC, Allan. Genesis, EDICEI Cap. 18, item 32
[172] XAVIER, Francisco C. The Messengers, Allan Kardec Educational Society, p. 24
[173] XAVIER, Francisco C. The Messengers, Allan Kardec Educational Society, p. 40
[174] XAVIER, Francisco C. The Messengers, Allan Kardec Educational Society, p. 41
[175] XAVIER, Francisco C. The Messengers, Allan Kardec Educational Society, p. 35
[176] XAVIER, Francisco C. The Messengers, Allan Kardec Educational Society, p. 24
[177] XAVIER, Francisco C. The Messengers, Allan Kardec Educational Society, p. 32
[178] XAVIER, Francisco C. Workers of the Life Eternal, EDICEI, p. 334
[179] XAVIER, Francisco C. Workers of the Life Eternal, EDICEI, p. 340
[180] XAVIER, Francisco C. Workers of the Life Eternal, EDICEI, p. 343
[181] XAVIER, Francisco C. Workers of the Life Eternal, EDICEI, p. 343
[182] KARDEC, Allan. The Spirits Book, White Crow Books, Question 1019, pp 522-524

[183] XAVIER, Francisco C. Workers of the Life Eternal, EDICEI, p. 240

[184] NDERF.org, "David G. - ADC", n.d., http://www.nderf.org/NDERF/NDE_Experiences/david_g_adc.htm , (accessed Aug. 1, 2014)

[185] NDERF.org, "David G. - ADC", n.d., http://www.nderf.org/NDERF/NDE_Experiences/david_g_adc.htm , (accessed Aug. 1, 2014)

[186] NDERF.org, "David G. - ADC", n.d., http://www.nderf.org/NDERF/NDE_Experiences/david_g_adc.htm , (accessed Aug. 1, 2014)

[187] NDERF.org, "David G. - ADC", n.d., http://www.nderf.org/NDERF/NDE_Experiences/david_g_adc.htm , (accessed Aug. 1, 2014)

[188] Swedenborg, E. A Swedenborg Sampler, Swedenborg Foundation Press, p 34

[189] Swedenborg, E. A Swedenborg Sampler, Swedenborg Foundation Press, p 34

[190] Swedenborg, E. A Swedenborg Sampler, Swedenborg Foundation Press, p 35

[191] Swedenborg, E. A Swedenborg Sampler, Swedenborg Foundation Press, p 35

[192] NDERF, Individual NDE Experiences – 3669 Gail, n.d., http://www.nderf.org/NDERF/NDE_Archives/NDERF_NDEs.htm (accessed June 28, 2014)

[193] Xavier, F.C. Liberation, EDICEI, pp. 53-54

[194] Xavier, F.C. Liberation, EDICEI, p. 54

[195] Xavier, F.C. Liberation, EDICEI, p. 56

[196] Xavier, F.C. Liberation, EDICEI, p. 57

[197] Xavier, F.C. Liberation, EDICEI, p. 58

[198] Xavier, F.C. Liberation, EDICEI, p. 59

[199] Kardec, A, Heaven and Hell, EDICEI, Part One - Chapter VII, pp. 131-132

[200] Kardec, A, Heaven and Hell, EDICEI, Part Two - Chapter VI, p. 437

[201] Xavier, F.C. Workers of the Life Eternal, EDICEI, p. 95

[202] Xavier, F.C. Nosso Lar, EDICEI, p. 17

[203] Pereira, Y. A. Memoirs of a Suicide, EDICEI, p. 46
[204]Pereira, Y. A. Memoirs of a Suicide, EDICEI, p. 47
[205] Xavier, F.C. Nosso Lar, EDICEI, pp. 74-75
[206] Xavier, F.C. Nosso Lar, EDICEI, p. 75
[207] Xavier, F.C. Nosso Lar, EDICEI, p. 76
[208] Xavier, F.C. Action and Reaction, EDICEI, p. 33

[209] en.wikipedia.org/wiki/Allan_Kardec
[210] KARDEC, Allan. The Spirits Book, White Crow Books, Question 1016, p xxx
[211] Xavier, F.C. Renunciation, EDICEI, pp. 26-27
[212] Xavier, F.C. Nossa Lar, EDICEI, p 53
[213] Xavier, F.C. Nossa Lar, EDICEI, p 54
[214] Xavier, F.C. Nossa Lar, EDICEI, p 55
[215] Xavier, F.C. Nossa Lar, EDICEI, p 64
[216] Xavier, F.C. Nossa Lar, EDICEI, pp. 69-70
[217] Xavier, F.C. Nossa Lar, EDICEI, p 80
[218] Xavier, F.C. Nossa Lar, EDICEI, p 132
[219] Xavier, F.C. Nossa Lar, EDICEI, p 226
[220] KARDEC, Allan, Heaven and Hell, EDICEI, Chap. 3 num. 12, p. 44
[221] Xavier, Francisco C., Nossa Lar, EDICEI, p.219
[222] Xavier, Francisco C., Nossa Lar, EDICEI, p.219
[223] Pereira, Y.A., Memoirs of the Suicide, EDICEI, p. 102
[224] Pereira, Y.A., Memoirs of the Suicide, EDICEI, pp. 102-103
[225] Xavier, Francisco C., Nossa Lar, EDICEI, p. 59
[226] Xavier, Francisco C., Nossa Lar, EDICEI, p. 60
[227] Xavier, F. C., On the Way to the Light, EDICEI, pp. 123-124
[228] Goldennuggetswebs, "Revelation", n.d., http://www.goldnuggetwebs.com/revelation/revelation-p2.html, (accessed September 7, 2014)
[229] Xavier, F. C., On the Way to the Light, EDICEI, pp. 124-125
[230] Xavier, F. C., On the Way to the Light, EDICEI, p. 125
[231] Kardec, A., The Spirits Book, White Crow Books, Ques. 1019, p. 522
[232] Kardec, A., The Spirits Book, White Crow Books, Ques. 1019, p. 523

[233] Kardec, Allan. Genesis, EDICEI Cap. 18, item 27

[234] Kardec, A., The Gospel According to Spiritism, EDICEI, p. 327

[235] XAVIER, Francisco C. Renunciation, EDICEI, p. 33

[236] KARDEC, Allan. The Gospel According to Spiritism, EDICEI, Chap. 3 num. 8, p 71

[237] KARDEC, Allan. The Gospel According to Spiritism, EDICEI, Chap. 3 num. 8, p 75

[238] KARDEC, Allan. The Spirits Book, White Crow Books, Question 182, p 147

[239] KARDEC, Allan. The Gospel According to Spiritism, EDICEI, Chap. 3 num. 8, p 72

[240] KARDEC, Allan. The Gospel According to Spiritism, EDICEI, Chap. 3 num. 8, p 73

[241] Xavier, Francisco C. On the Way to the Light, EDICEI, p.180

[242] Xavier, Francisco C. On the Way to the Light, EDICEI, p.192

[243] Xavier, Francisco C. On the Way to the Light, EDICEI, p.169

[244] KARDEC, Allan. Genesis, EDICEI Cap. 16, item 63

[245] KARDEC, Allan. Genesis, EDICEI Cap. 18, item 27

[246] KARDEC, Allan. Genesis, EDICEI Cap. 16, item 13

[247]KARDEC, Allan. The Spirits Book, White Crow Books, Question 536, p 304

[248]XAVIER, Francisco C. The Messengers, Allan Kardec Educational Society, p. 176

[249] KARDEC, Allan. The Spirits Book, White Crow Books, Question 781, p 402

[250] XAVIER, Francisco C. The Messengers, Allan Kardec Educational Society, p. 180

[251] XAVIER, Francisco C. The Messengers, Allan Kardec Educational Society, p. 180

[252] XAVIER, Francisco C. The Messengers, Allan Kardec Educational Society, p. 180

[253] XAVIER, Francisco C. The Messengers, Allan Kardec Educational Society, pp. 180-180

[254] Colorado State University, "CNG Garden Notes", n.d., http://www.ext.colostate.edu/mg/gardennotes/231.html, (accessed October 11, 2014)

[255] KARDEC, Allan. The Spirits Book, White Crow Books, Question 710, p 377

[256] NDERF.org, "William H NDE", n.d., http://www.nderf.org/NDERF/NDE_Experiences/william_h_nde_7340.htm, (accessed Dec. 31, 2014)

[257] NDERF.org, "William H NDE", n.d., http://www.nderf.org/NDERF/NDE_Experiences/william_h_nde_7340.htm, (accessed Dec. 31, 2014)

[258] NDERF.org, "William H NDE", n.d., http://www.nderf.org/NDERF/NDE_Experiences/william_h_nde_7340.htm, (accessed Dec. 31, 2014)

[259]NDERF.org, "William H NDE", n.d., http://www.nderf.org/NDERF/NDE_Experiences/william_h_nde_7340.htm, (accessed Dec. 31, 2014)

[260] NDERF.org, "William H NDE", n.d., http://www.nderf.org/NDERF/NDE_Experiences/william_h_nde_7340.htm, (accessed Dec. 31, 2014)

Made in the USA
Lexington, KY
06 October 2015